EMERGING
LEADERS

DAVE WILLIAMS

EMERGING LEADERS

A New

Breed

of Church

Leadership

for the

21st Century

DAVE WILLIAMS

EMERGING LEADERS

A New Breed Of Church Leadership For The 21st Century

Unless otherwise noted, Scripture quotations are taken from the King James Version of the Bible.

Scripture quotations marked (TLB) are taken from *The Living Bible* copyright © 1971. Used by permission of Tyndale House Publishers, Inc., Wheaton, IL 60189. All rights reserved.

Copyright © 2005 by Dr. David R. Williams

ISBN 0-938020-79-X

First Printing 2005

Cover By: Robison Gamble Creative

Published by

DECAPOLIS
PUBLISHING

Printed in the United States of America

BOOKS BY DAVE WILLIAMS

OTHER BOOKS BY DAVE WILLIAMS

CONTENTS

You will advance in
your calling by years, just
as if you pushed a fast
forward button.

FIRST THOUGHTS

God has given *you* a call and a destiny. It has never been more important that you carry it out purposefully. We live in perilous times and high-risk days which are leading up to the final moments of history.

Time is about up.

The countdown has begun, and soon the world will enter its deepest hour of agony, a time of unparalleled terror and anguish. Jesus said:

> And except those days should be shortened, there should no flesh be saved...
>
> —Matthew 24:22a

But *high-risk* days are also *high-opportunity* days for the Church. And I see an emerging breed of leaders stepping up to the challenge. They baffle leaders of the previous generation. They are simple men and women with remarkable faith. They seem to be cut from a different mold; sort of like from another world. They are a new breed of Christian leader — they are rising up by the tens of thousands right now as you read this. Perhaps you are one of them.

Their ears are tuned to Heaven's frequency. They're winners and not whiners; pacesetters and not puppets. They handle conflicts and challenges with incredible grace and strength.

I've observed them rising now — the new breed — emerging leaders for the 21st century.

Let me give you a snapshot of this new breed of leader here:

1. They march only to the Commander-In-Chief's (Jesus') orders.

2. They are incredibly creative and fresh, even unconventional, in their approach to life, work, evangelism, and ministry.

3. They take God at His Word, and apply strategic action. They are doers, not just hearers.

4. They don't wait until they feel "perfect" before they do something.

5. They are willing to leave everything to follow the will of God.

6. They don't fear going into new territories where others are afraid to go.

7. They understand and flow under true spiritual authority.

8. They practice the art of fasting, coupled with prayer.

9. They nurture and cherish the anointing of the Holy Spirit.

10. They really believe that with God all things are possible, and it is demonstrated in their vision and their action.

11. They refuse to be distracted from their God-given mission regardless of obstacles, resistence, misunderstandings, and ridicule.

12. They cannot tolerate hypocrisy. As a result, they are torturously honest and sincere, even when it means becoming vulnerable themselves.

13. They are quick to repent when the Lord points out a site of disobedience.

14. They deplore programs that have no purpose and produce no fruit.

15. They are reliable, dependable, and incredibly loyal but have little patience with legalism and nit-picky policies.

16. They speak well of ministers and leaders who are not of their own group. They fear grieving the Holy Spirit with their words. They have renounced sins of the tongue.

17. They walk by faith, not by sight. They "see" the invisible and employ their faith, action, and perseverance to bring it into the visible.

18. They are not afraid to roll up their sleeves, get down in the dirt, and make disciples for Jesus.

19. They are zealous for the honor of God and deplore false teaching.

20. They seem to have endless energy, never stressing out or burning out, because they've learned the

secret of true anointing and the blessing of casting their cares upon Jesus.

21. They are amazingly tenacious, persistent and sometimes seemingly violent — forceful — in their commitment to press on amidst conflict and obstacles.

22. They walk confidently in a modern day prophetic anointing.

23. They hate sin with an almost rebellious-like passion. They rebel against sin and demonic temptations.

24. They are humble and servant-hearted.

25. They have a strong Christ-centeredness and cannot tolerate pride, hypocrisy, insincerity and lack of genuineness.

26. They know what they want and it is in perfect harmony with what God wants.

27. They love sinners.

28. They know how to rest, relax and have fun. Their life is an adventure, and they don't feel guilty about it.

Old school leaders who refuse a fresh change — not in doctrines or theology, but in obedience to a "present word" from the Lord — will be left in the dust as the new breed of emerging leaders run for the prize of the high calling in Christ Jesus.

Don't criticize them. Don't even try to figure them out. They are different.

I had lunch with a young man named Jerome. Twenty-three years old and he's a new breed of emerging leader in the twenty-first-century. I've watched his progress ever since he met Jesus two years ago, and have been impressed with his spiritual caliber. Jerome doesn't particulary care for hip-hop music. But God spoke to him and told him to learn the hip-hop culture to reach people for Christ.

Jerome gathered a team, made a recording, and started ministering at youth gatherings and other hot spots wherever there was an open door. He sings his rap, gives altar calls, and scores of young people come to Christ. This young emerging leader has a strategic plan. He's under spiritual authority and is achieving what God called him to do. Don't criticize him just because you don't understand his methods.

Many in this new breed of emerging leaders are going to baffle the current leaders with their supernatural strategies and God-anointed methodologies.

In the chapters that follow, I'll lay out the character traits of emerging twenty-first-century leaders of the Church of Jesus Christ. We'll look at discouragement, distractions, and other challenges leaders face. When we're through, you will have advanced in your calling by years, just as if you pushed a fast forward button. You'll skip over problems that once would have dragged you down. You'll change the way you approach leadership at all levels.

For additional help, each chapter is followed by three Power Points which will help you distill and digest the truths we've just learned.

I pray the powerful insights in the pages ahead will equip you to fulfill your highest destiny in Christ as a twenty-first-century leader. These are days of unmatched opportunity. Let's get going!

Dave Williams

Lansing, Michigan

FIRST THOUGHTS

There is a hunger that can only be satisfied by sharing the Gospel and introducing people to Christ.

CHAPTER 1

EMERGING LEADERS KNOW THEIR CALLING AND ARE ESTABLISHED IN IT

I could hardly believe the statistic I heard quoted during a meeting of leading ministers.[1] In all Christian denominations, we were told: Thirty-seven out of forty pastors drop out of the ministry at some point during their life. *Thirty-seven out of forty* don't go the distance but instead leave the pulpits to sell insurance, or cars, or carpeting, or establish some career outside their ministry calling. That amounts to a potential of 5,000 ministers a month leaving the ministry!

I was astounded. At the same time I could visualize the invasion of other religions into our country: the mosques and tem-

1   Meeting of the General Presbyters, General Council of the Assemblies of God, August 2002, Springfield, MO

ples going up all over the place, the millions of lost and spiritually bereft people whose American dream had not satisfied their deepest longings. And yet only three out of every forty ministers who are called to the ministry actually fulfill their call! Only three stick with the message of hope, plow the hard ground, and spend their lives working in the harvest field.

That's a terribly sad statistic, but *it's also reversible!*

MINISTERS IN MOTHBALLS

It doesn't have to be true of you! As a leader, maybe you've been beaten up in the ministry. Maybe you've thought of dropping out of the race. You know the trials leaders face that nobody else has to deal with. It reminds me of when I was in the Navy and stationed in San Diego. There was a ship graveyard where decommissioned ships went to be stripped down. It was a massive place with dozens of gargantuan ocean vessels waiting to be dismantled. Workers spent months taking everything of value off those ships, and then the ships were docked and mothballed. At that point, a ship was inspected to see if it should be sold for scrap or someday be recommissioned and put back into active service.

Ministers who have left the ministry feel stripped of value, ineffective, with nothing left to give.

Ministers who've left the ministry are like those ships. They feel stripped of value, ineffective, with nothing left to give. They feel they've been put out to pasture, stuck in some graveyard where nobody cares about their work anymore. But God knows their true value, and it is great! He has a plan to recommission those "old ships" and put them back into active service. God has a plan to restore men and women to their pulpits. Better yet, He has a plan to establish you in your call *so you don't leave in the first place.*

CHAFF OR WHEAT?

One of the Scriptures closest to my heart is Jeremiah 23:28-29. That chapter talks about false prophets, with whom God is upset, but tucked right in the middle of His rebuke are these words:

> The prophet that hath a dream, let him tell a dream; and he that hath my word, let him speak my word faithfully. What *is* the chaff to the wheat? saith the LORD. *Is* not my word like as a fire? saith the LORD; and like a hammer *that* breaketh the rock in pieces?

I love those words, "He that hath My Word, let him speak My Word faithfully." They point to the first characteristic of today's emerging new leaders: *They know their call and are established in it.* They don't meander or go in circles. They don't worry about what other ministers are doing or people here or there following ministry fads. They don't get distracted or burned out and towed to the ship graveyard to become one of the devil's decaying trophies. Emerging leaders are established in what God has called them to do and who He has called them to be. Friend, that is *your* destiny!

GOD'S CALL TO MY HEART

I want you to know that I have been through ministry trials and successes, just as you have. I have seen both sides of the coin since that day in 1975 when I was filled with the Holy Spirit and my life was radically changed. From then on I wanted desperately to win souls. I possessed a hunger that could only be satisfied by sharing the Gospel and introducing people to Christ. I started sensing God's call to leadership and ministry. I worked at a power plant then, but instead of driving to work, I'd walk and preach every step of the way. I'd even preach to the squirrels. After all, Jesus said to preach the Gospel to every creature (Mark 16:15), and squirrels are creatures. I memorized an old Rex Humbard sermon called, "You can get what you want, but you may not want what you're gonna get." Whenever I saw a squirrel, I'd lay that line on him: "You can get what you want, but you ain't gonna want what you get!" I'm quite certain a lot of squirrels were saved under my ministry!

God has a plan to restore men and women to their pulpits.

I had a terrific job at the power plant and was advancing rapidly. I had great job security and a good paycheck, but it all seemed mundane and bland. All I could think about was ministering and preaching. But I didn't know if God had called me to full-time ministry, and I didn't want to launch something that was just my own ambition.

My frustration grew to the point where I thought I'd break in half. I had to find out what my call was, so I went into my living room in my little bachelor house and prayed, "God, I'm going to pray until You tell me what You want me to do with my life." I knelt down and prayed in the Spirit for twenty, thirty, forty minutes, maybe an hour. Then something happened that had never happened before. I felt a bubbling up from inside of me, and I spoke forth these prophetic words, "David, I've called you to speak My Word and to speak it faithfully. The prophet that hath a dream let him tell his dream. But you have My Word. Speak My Word faithfully. What is the chaff to the wheat?" I got up from that time of prayer, and from that moment on, I have never doubted my call. I'd heard from God.

TURNING THE CALL INTO ACTION

You could probably relate a similar story, perhaps more exciting than mine, about how God called you to the ministry or a leadership role. Perhaps you were like me in those early days when I had just received my calling: I had an invitation but no road map. I knew *where* I wanted to go but not *how* to get there. I decided to start a Bible study in my home. One person, and only one person, showed up week after week, but I kept with it. I asked the Lord how to get more people to come. I read this in His Word:

> Go ye therefore, and teach all nations...
>
> —Matthew 28:19

So I obeyed that word to "Go." I noticed some young men playing on the basketball court across the street from my house. Without thinking, I yelled over to them, "Hey, would you guys like to get saved?" They came across the street to my little house and asked, "What?" I repeated, "Saved. Have you ever heard about being saved?" They didn't know what I was talking about, so I explained how Jesus died on the Cross and rose from the dead. I told them that if they received Him, they could be saved and go to Heaven someday. Six of the seven guys said, "I'd like that." They bowed their heads in my little living room and prayed to receive Jesus. Now I had seven people in my Bible study.

Then, one day, I was riding a Greyhound bus from South Bend, Indiana, and a lady next to me started asking questions. I pulled out my Bible to give her some answers. Somehow I seemed to remember exactly where the right Scriptures were that she needed to hear. Soon, another person turned around and asked a question, so I looked in the Bible and answered it. Somebody else got out of his seat and came over to ask a question. The next thing I knew, there was a crowd gathered around me on the bus, and I was answering with truths from the Bible! Finally the driver said, "You all have to get back into your seats." So I wrote out my address for all of them and invited them to come to my house if they had more questions.

About twenty minutes after I got home that night, there was a knock at the door. There stood one of the people from the bus, saying, "Hi, I was on that bus, and I still have questions." One by one others came, and in a short time they started receiving Jesus and being filled with the Holy Spirit. One girl said, "I have to go get my boyfriend." Thirty minutes later, she was back with her boyfriend asking if he could get saved too. He did. A mother fetched her daughter; friends convinced friends, and soon I had twenty-four people in my Bible study.

But I still wasn't exclusively in the ministry. I had my job at the power plant. I loved my work there but wanted to work for God full-time.

I attended a seminar at Christ For The Nations in Dallas, Texas, with my new wife Mary Jo. We were seeking direction from the Lord. There we met Chuck Flynn, who people said was a prophet. At that time, I'd never heard of modern-day prophets. Chuck said he would prophesy over us the way Paul prophesied over Timothy, but he'd wait until after the service. So Mary Jo and I and two of our friends waited in line. Sincere but scared, we wondered what would happen when it was our turn.

Emerging leaders are established in what God has called them to do and who He has called them to be.

Mary Jo and I didn't know what would become of my desire to preach, which was growing stronger by the day. Chuck stood before me and said, "Young man, I'm sensing there is coming a change to your ministry. God is saying don't be afraid of it. You'll go through a time of challenge and a time where you'll be tempted to be discouraged. People will come against you, but stick with the call." He prophesied over Mary Jo and our friends too.

Mary Jo and I returned to Lansing, and within days my pastor called me and asked if I would like to be on his staff. I agreed, and before long I was his assistant, and he took me under his wing, discipled me, and told me about all the "glories" of pastoring. Then one day he said to me, "Every church I've pastored fell apart after I left. I don't want it to happen to this one. This will probably be my last church. I don't want the congregation to know this, but I'm going to retire in a year. I was hoping that, if it was God's will, the people would select you as the pastor and the church wouldn't fall apart."

God has called you. He will establish you.

It happened as he hoped. One year and nineteen days later, I became the pastor. This 143-pound untrained "green bean" became pastor of Mount Hope Church. I didn't know how to pastor. I didn't have a clue. I looked out in the pews on Sunday morning and saw people who were smarter, older, saved longer, filled with the Holy Spirit longer, and flowed in the Spirit better than me. I was scared, but I knew one thing: God had called me. I knew He would establish me, just as He had promised in that verse in Jeremiah. And that led me to understand the second characteristic of an effective leader, which we'll talk about next.

POWER POINT:

1. *Do you know what your call is? Describe it in 1 or 2 sentences.*

2. *How did God call you to be a leader? What events surrounded that transformation? Relate them briefly, as an encouragement to yourself.*

3. *Do you have trouble remembering that God Himself will establish you in your call? Which Bible verses encourage you? Describe the kind of leader you want to be; then lay out a simple plan on how you can be more firmly established in your call.*

*Y*ou can be faithful and
established in the call God
has put on your life, neither
being ashamed nor impatient.

2
CHAPTER

EMERGING LEADERS ARE FAITHFUL TO GOD AND TO THEIR CALLING

If you are like me, your first steps in leadership weren't glamorous. I probably wasn't the type of leader the people of Mount Hope Church had envisioned. I hadn't attended Bible school. I had been an assistant pastor for just over a year, and I had little theological training or practical ministry experience. I was from the same town and had worked a regular job just like everyone else. Why would they be impressed by me?

I knew I was in over my head, so I did the only thing I knew to do: I came in and prayed at 5:30 every morning at the altar, asking God to help me. During that time I began to grasp the second characteristic of an effective twenty-first-century leader, which is embodied in this verse:

Faithful *is* he that calleth you, who also will do *it*.

—1 Thessalonians 5:24

As I began to take my first few steps in leading the church body, this principle stuck with me: *If He called you, He will do it. And if He will do it, you can be faithful to that call.* That truth came alive to me.

As a leader, you don't have to jump from here to there, one church or ministry to another, trying to find fulfillment or success, climbing some "ministry ladder." You can be faithful and established in the call God has put on your life, neither being ashamed nor impatient.

Emerging leaders are faithful in their calling. They aren't quitters. They are stable, steady, and in this race for the long term. You can be faithful to your original calling in spite of life's distractions, challenges, questions, and obstacles.

In my case, money was my first challenge in the pastorate. I had to decide I was going to serve God and not mammon. The church was only paying me forty-two cents an hour for the first six weeks — $25 a week for sixty hours of work. Mary Jo and I thought we were in Heaven when they raised my pay to $2 an hour. But we had to examine our financial and spiritual priorities and make some decisions. By keeping this principle in mind, we made those decisions based *not* on money but on the call. Here's what we decided:

- **NUMBER ONE:** Mary Jo would not work outside the home but would stay home with our two children.

- **NUMBER TWO:** We would always give God at least 10 percent of our gross income as a tithe and 10 percent as an offering, 20 percent total.

- **NUMBER THREE:** We would pay our bills on time and in full, trusting God to be faithful to us as we were faithful to Him.

- **NUMBER FOUR:** We would never tell any person, other than God, about our personal needs. We would instead be concerned about other people's needs.

We clung to those guiding principles even when I was earning only 42 cents an hour in those early years of ministry. And we still stick to those principles today. We had to pay our own taxes, our own Social Security, and for a while the church wanted us to buy our own health insurance. This put a huge financial strain on us, but Mary Jo and I decided that we would live in a cardboard box in the public park, if necessary, in order to follow the call of God. As it turned out, we didn't have to live in the park, but we did live in an "interesting" neighborhood for many years. Policemen from our church would drive

Emerging leaders are faithful in their calling. They aren't quitters. They are stable and steady.

through the neighborhood to see if we were alright. They couldn't understand why I lived there, but they didn't know we were being paid below the national poverty level. We lived in that neighborhood because it was within our means and because we were being faithful to God, counting on Him being faithful to us. We wouldn't seek answers or success anywhere else but through Him.

> *Faithfulness is the difference between those who are merely called and those who are called and chosen.*

We were *faithful* to our calling, just as emerging leaders are today.

THE BRIDGE BETWEEN BEING CALLED AND BEING CHOSEN

You have been called by God to break open new territory and to give direction to the Church. You must see new horizons, new vistas, to see the heart of God and to lead God's people in turning them into reality.

But have you ever wondered at this verse?

> For many are called, but few *are* chosen.

> —Matthew 22:14

Why are many called but few chosen? Who decides which ones are called and which ones are chosen? And what happens to people *between* the calling and the choosing? Why do some make it and others drop out, fizzle out, and freak out? I struggled with this for a long time, and then God gave me an answer.

There is always a bridge between "the call" and "the choosing."

There is always a bridge between a promise and a provision.

There is always a bridge between a dream and that dream becoming a reality.

There is always a bridge between the anointing and the appointing.

What is that bridge? It is *faithfulness*. Faithfulness is the difference between those who are merely called and those who are called *and* chosen.

> *Faithfulness is tenacity, perseverance, hang-in-there power.*

Emerging leaders are extraordinary in their faithfulness.

Faithfulness is tenacity, perseverance, hanging-in-there power. To get from being called to being chosen, you must be faithful, and the only way to be faithful is when you are *established* in your call.

The good news is, anyone can be faithful. I'm so glad that Jesus won't someday say, "Well done, thou good and prophetic servant." I can be faithful, even when I don't know exactly how to be prophetic. He won't say, "Well done, thou good and wild charismatic servant." I would love to be a wild charismatic servant and dance before the Lord the way some people do, but I'd probably look ridiculous. I'm glad He didn't say, "Well done, thou good and handsome servant." That would disqualify me right away!

Rather, He will say, "Well done, thou good and *faithful* servant" (Matthew 25:21). That puts us all on the same playing field because everybody can be faithful to the call in which they are established. That means you can too!

When we are established in our calling and we have the faith that God will do it, we can relax and enjoy the bridge between the calling and the choosing. Oh, it can be a frustrating bridge when you have to hang in there through the challenges, through the tough times; when people are calling you names, when there are rumors, gossip, and church trouble. As a leader, you probably already know what these situations are like.

Faithfulness leads to great rewards that lie just on the other side of the tough times.

A pastor's sons were fighting with each other when their father told them to stop. They turned to him and said, "We're just playing church."

Another man was rescued from an isolated island in the middle of the Pacific where he was stranded alone. He hadn't seen another human being in months. His rescuers saw three huts he had built, so they asked, "What are those huts?" The man replied, "This is the hut I live in. This other hut is the church I go to on Sunday." They questioned, "What about that third hut?" He said, "Oh, that's the church I *used* to attend."

As leaders, we know what that's like! Strife and dissension comes with the territory, but even the worst times won't shake us from our faithfulness when we know that we've been established in our calling.

PEA PATCH FAITH

There's a terrific example of a faithful leader in the Old Testament. An army private in David's military named Shammah was told to guard a pea patch. (You can read more about him in 2 Samuel 23:11-12.) Shammah was on the lowest rung of authority in David's military, but the Bible says not to despise the day of small beginnings (Zechariah 4:10). Shammah and other Hebrew soldiers were suddenly attacked by the Philistines who wanted the king's pea patch. The other Hebrew soldiers ran off, but Shammah said to himself, "I was called to guard this patch, so I can be faithful in that call because faithful is He that called me." Instead of turning tail and running like the others. The Bible says, "...he struck the Philistines." Now, when an army would attack, they usually had as many as 800 men. Can you imagine having *that* kind of faithfulness?

It would have been easy for him to say, "This is just a pea patch. Am I going to lose my life over it? Certainly, the king wouldn't expect me to die for a pea patch." With that attitude he would have stayed at the rank of private all of his life. Instead, through faithfulness, he single-handedly destroyed all those Philistine enemies, protected the king's pea patch as ordered, and as a result was promoted to one of the top ranking generals. He became one of David's "top three." Overnight, he went from private to national leader. He was honored and respected throughout the entire land. He received wealth, was blessed and exalted. Why? Because he was smarter or more daring or better than the others? No. It's because he was faithful. He hung in there when the going got tough. The Bible says:

> **For a just *man* falleth seven times, and riseth up again...**
>
> **—Proverbs 24:16a**

Shammah is an example for you. Faithfulness leads to great rewards that lie just on the other side of the tough times.

John Garlock read a poem at Christ For The Nations Institute years ago that I enjoy. It's called "Two Frogs."

> *Two frogs fell into a can of cream, or so it has been told;*
>
> *The sides of the can were shiny and steep; the cream was deep and cold;*
>
> *"Oh, what's the use," said number one, "it's plain no help is around. Good-bye my friend, good-bye sad world," and weeping still he drowned.*
>
> *But number two, of sterner stuff, dog paddled in surprise;*

As he licked his creamy lips and blinked his creamy eyes;

"I'll swim at least awhile," he thought, or so it has been said;

"The world couldn't possibly be a better place if one more frog were dead."

So for an hour or more he kicked and swam, and not once did he stop to mutter;

Then he hopped out by the island he'd made of fresh churned butter.²

TESTS OF FAITHFULNESS

I have known that feeling of "I think I'm going to drown, there are so many problems!" Maybe you have too. All you can do is hang in there and kick like the frog and fight like Shammah. My first test of faithfulness in ministry came early. As a young pastor I was seeking God's vision for our church. Early one morning I was at the church praying when God popped a Scripture off the page and into my heart. It was Acts 13:44.

> **And the next sabbath day came almost the whole city together to hear the word of God.**

In that moment, I saw that it was God's will for an entire city to attend church on the Sabbath day, hearing the Word of God. That became my vision for Mount Hope Church. (I'm convinced that God will give you similar vision and specific direction.)

---

2   Garlock, Rev. John, CFNI, *The Power of Tenacity*, 1977, Dallas, TX

For the next few years, our church grew steadily. We progressed to five Sunday services. Attendance jumped from 225 to 1,200 people. But the people who had been in the church for a long time, whose fathers and grandfathers had been founding members, started feeling that they had lost control.

We launched a building program for a 3,000-seat facility, and that's when I first felt the ominous undercurrents of dissent. These church controllers sent rumors out like foxes in the grain fields. I didn't know what was happening or where these ideas were coming from. One rumor suggested, "Maybe we have a Jim Jones (meaning me) on our hands." Then people held secret "prayer and gossip" meetings that I heard about secondhand.

Feeling beat up, I went into one of our Sunday school rooms and fasted and prayed. I prayed, "Lord, I need to hear from You on this building program. I don't care if we go to twelve services in this building. It doesn't matter to me. Just tell me what we should do." God assured me that His plan was for us to construct a new building.

"But," He said to my heart through the Scriptures, "don't go to the bank and borrow money for it." I replied, "That's not my decision; that's the Board's decision." The Lord spoke to my heart and said, "I am not holding the Board responsible for obeying Me on this matter. I'm holding *you* responsible. I've made *you* the overseer, the pastor, the one with the big picture."

So I gathered the board members together and told them we wouldn't go to the bank to borrow money. *Whomph!* You would have thought I'd said a curse word. "We've gone to the bank and borrowed money for everything we've done," they asserted. "Borrowing is an act of faith. You have the faith that the payment will be there." I countered that I'd fasted and prayed and God had spoken to my heart and told me not to borrow from the bank to build this $6.2 million facility. They asked, reasonably, "Where are we going to get the money if we don't borrow it?" I said I didn't know.

They tried to push me into a decision of disobedience. The man who was the biggest influence in the church and who had relatives in every department — I called him the Godfather, the leader of the "Christian Mafia" — came to my office, sat down, and said, "We've got to get that church built. We're becoming the laughingstock of the community because the big sign out there says, 'Future home of Mount Hope Church.' Now the weeds are growing up, and nothing is going on."

I told him I didn't think we were the laughingstock of the community just because we weren't going to borrow money. Then he pulled out the big guns. "My father founded this church," he said. "We have always gone to the bank. We've got a good relationship with the bank. They're willing to loan us money." I felt somewhat intimidated. This man was much older than I, and I had always looked up to him. I told him the Lord had let me know that if we borrowed money from the bank, He would never bring Mount Hope Church to the glory He intended for it. "I feel like I'd be disobeying if I signed for a loan from the bank," I said.

He retorted, "I know all that, but do it anyway. There'll be problems for a while, but after a few years it will all be forgotten."

"You're asking me to disobey God?" I inquired.

"It will work out. Sure, there'll be ripples, but it will all smooth out over time. If you don't borrow the money, a lot of people are going to be leaving the church and taking their tithe money with them."

God will build inside you a sense of call so strong that no circumstance will be able to knock you down.

"Who?" I asked.

"My family, for one, and the people we influence," he said.

Like Shammah, I faced a decision. Would I run away based on a threat, or would I stand my ground in faith? For the first time I realized I was the God-ordained pastor, the chief executive officer, the chairman of the board. I was the overseer of the church. I was not merely the Sunday morning chaplain to be pushed around by bullies.

I stood my ground, showed that man the door, and one hundred people left the church with him. Like Shammah, one by one, I had to stand up to them. It broke my heart. They took their tithe money, but the month after they left, the church income went up by $10,000 a week! I had been promoted by God to a new place of leadership effectiveness. Church attendance went up faster than ever. I said, "God, how can this happen?" I knew the answer was faithfulness; going from the calling to the choosing by hanging in there.

Maybe you're a pastor who's secretly looking for other jobs or other pastorates so you can get out of your present, painful circumstances. I believe God can turn the world right side up, right where you're at now. *But you've got to stand up to the tough stuff.*

Know that God will establish you if you'll just stick with Him and with your call. You're going to find yourself chosen for great success, victory, power, and anointing in this twenty-first century. God will build inside you a sense of call so strong that no circumstance, no situation will be able to knock you down.

No matter how discouraged you are, you *can* be an effective twenty-first-century leader! As someone who has been there, I challenge you to stick to your calling and be faithful. He will establish you in your calling even when the situation looks bleak. Victory is around the next corner!

There's a third trait leaders possess that can bring revelation, deliverance, and greater miracles.

Power Points:

1. *What has been your time of greatest testing as a leader? How were you faithful during that time? Recount the situation briefly.*

2. *What challenges do you face right now as a leader?*

3. *Write a plan of action. How can you stay faithful to your calling through these present challenges?*

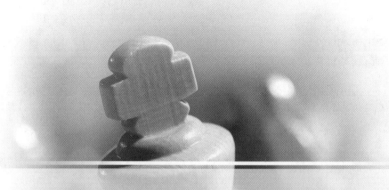

*One of the most overlooked
ways to be a faithful and
effective leader is through
fasting and prayer.*

CHAPTER

EMERGING LEADERS PRACTICE THE DISCIPLINE OF FASTING

The subject of this chapter may surprise you, but I want to show you how fasting can be a critical part of an effective leader's lifestyle. Without it, some potentially great leaders wander from their purpose or become unfocused and out of touch with God. Fasting is a bedrock practice of people who do great things for God. If you are to be faithful and established in your call, you need to fast, at least occasionally.

In 1999, I attended a retirement banquet for Loren Triplett who for eight years was Director of Foreign Missions for the Assemblies of God.[3] I had served on the missions board

---

3   University Plaza, Loren Triplett banquet, November 1999, Springfield, MO

for three years and came to greatly respect and love Loren. As I thought back, I realized that our denomination had almost doubled the number of nations where we sent missionaries under his leadership. When Loren began we were in eighty-six nations. Eight years later we were in 156 more nations. We grew almost as much in eight years as we had in the previous seventy-five.

As I was wondering how Loren had led such a surge, I fell into conversation with his son Don, a missionary to Central America. Don told me, "My father lives a fasted life. He fasts continually, maybe two days a week." On Christmas day, while most people were having dinner, the Triplett family was fasting and taking Communion around the Christmas tree. Don had adopted that lifestyle too and was in the habit of going up into the mountain caves of Nicaragua to fast for three days, praying and getting God's guidance. Through the vision God gave him for King's Castle and other ministries, Don has already reached 2.5 million people for Jesus Christ in his young life!

Fasting is a bedrock practice of people who do great things for God.

One of the most overlooked ways to be a faithful and effective leader is through fasting and prayer. The Bible shouts to us about its importance. Elijah fasted forty days. Moses fasted forty days. Jesus fasted forty days. Paul fasted often. In the book of Joel, fasting was God's remedy for the problem of planting much and reaping little.

> Sanctify ye a fast, call a solemn assembly, gather the elders and the inhabitants of the land into the house of the LORD your God, and cry unto the LORD.
>
> —Joel 1:14

The city of Nineveh in Assyria fasted and prayed, and God withheld His judgment because of it.

> So the people of Nineveh believed God, and proclaimed a fast, and put on sackcloth, from the greatest of them even to the least of them.
>
> —Jonah 3:5

The Jewish race was spared in the days of Esther because they called a corporate fast.

> Go, gather together all the Jews that are present in Shushan, and fast ye for me, and neither eat nor drink three days, night or day: I also and my maidens will fast likewise; and so I will go in unto the king, which is not according to the law: and if I perish, I perish.
>
> —Esther 4:16

In Acts 10, Cornelius wasn't even a believer, but he noticed this practice of the Jews called fasting. Though he was a Gentile, he fasted. One day while he was fasting, an angel appeared to him. The angel told Cornelius to send for Peter, who told him about the Gospel. Cornelius was saved and filled with the Holy Spirit, and his whole family was saved in one day! What did he do to initiate it? He fasted.

Emerging leaders in the twenty-first century live a fasted life, denying themselves, taking up their crosses, and following Jesus who said, "*when* you fast," not "*if* you fast" (Matthew 6:16).

Let's look at three miracles that flow from this amazing practice called fasting.

SPIRITUAL MIRACLES OF FASTING

Fasting can bring a series of miracles to our lives. The first is a spiritual miracle. When the disciples couldn't cast out a demon, Jesus said:

> **Howbeit this kind goeth not out but by prayer and fasting.**

> —Matthew 17:21

Sometimes prayer alone isn't the answer. You need fasting too to see spiritual miracles.

I know a pastor whose wife walked away from the ministry. She started gambling, playing Bingo, and skipping church. He still came to church Sunday after Sunday, preaching his heart out, but his helpmate wasn't with him. She had no regard for the things of God. This pastor finally said, "I'm going to fast for my wife." He started a forty-day fast, and after just seven days of that fast, something scared his wife into coming to church. When her husband gave the altar call, she was the first one there repenting and making things right with God.

Fasting is God's remedy for the problem of planting much and reaping little.

That's a spiritual miracle!

Dr. James Hammil pastored a great church in Memphis, Tennessee. One day, years ago, he got a bad report from the doctor: He was full of cancer and wasn't going to live six months. His church board took action. They went before the church and said, "Friends, doctors say our pastor is full of cancer and is going to die. We need to fast and pray. We can't afford to lose him." That church fasted and prayed for their pastor, and God healed every square inch of his body. He went on to live a long and effective life as a leader.

Emerging leaders in the twenty-first century live a fasted life.

The first-century church surged with explosive growth into village after village, and the Holy Spirit supernaturally guided them. No leader was selected or ordained without fasting and prayer. Acts 13 tells us they were worshiping the Lord with fasting and prayer, and the Holy Spirit said to separate Paul and Barnabas for His work.

> As they ministered to the Lord, and fasted, the Holy Ghost said, Separate me Barnabas and Saul for the work whereunto I have called them.
>
> —Acts 13:2

When they had fasted and prayed, they laid hands on them and sent them on the mission.

A few years ago our church needed two new deacons. We prayed and fasted and asked God who He wanted to fill those slots. I was preaching on a Sunday night, and I looked over the congregation. Way in the back I saw two faces that looked like they were lit up and glowing from the inside. It was almost distracting. Every time I looked, their faces jumped out at me, and the Lord spoke to me and said, "There are your new deacons." Those men went on to serve full, productive terms on our deacon board. What a blessing they were to me and our church.

Jesus said, "when" you fast, not "if" you fast.

A man named George McClusky fasted daily. He denied himself, took up his cross, and fasted his lunch every day. He spent the time praying for his grandchildren. As a result, every one of his grandchildren became preachers. The granddaughters married preachers, and all the boys became preachers, except for one. His name is Dr. James Dobson.[4]

Fasting helps recapture our hunger for God. God releases spiritual power into our lives. It doesn't make God love us more. That's impossible to do. Neither does fasting build our faith; only the Word does that. But fasting seems to get us into a position to receive more power from God, so we experience more miracles. As leaders we need all the power that God will entrust to us.

These are the first major rewards of fasting: deeper spiritual perception, a fresh power with God, and a recapturing of our heart that may have drifted away.

---

4 Dobson, James C., Dr., *Straight Talk To Men And Their Wives*, p. 53-55, 1980, Key-Word Books, Waco, TX, ISBN 0-8499-4165-2

REWARD OF A HEALTHY MIND

The next reward is a healthy mind. Anything that's out of control is dangerous — a car, an airplane, spending, government, a temper. Many live out of control because they are slaves to their schedules, slaves to the television and to other people's interests. But fasting humbles the soul. David said:

> ...I humbled my soul with fasting...
>
> —Psalm 35:13b

Fasting gives our mind new adequacy and poise. It scares away the emotional and intellectual cockroaches that lurk in our mental crawl spaces. When you fast, it's easy to get torturously honest before the Lord. Religion makes you forget how to be real with God. It consists of a public show and making impressions. But with fasting, there's no public show and no impression. Everything gets real.

David Yonggi Cho's church in Seoul, South Korea, has 800,000 members and is the largest church in the world. Some historians say it's the largest single church in history. You might think the counseling load would be outrageous, but it's not because their rule is simple: if you come for counseling, you get five minutes to tell what the problem is. The

In the first-century church, no leader was selected or ordained without fasting and prayer.

solution is always the same: fast and pray three days at Prayer Mountain. If someone comes back after three days of fasting and prayer and says it didn't work, their new "prescription" is ten days of fasting and prayer. If ten days don't work, they prescribe thirty days. Nobody ever comes back for counseling! Why? Either they don't want to fast anymore, or their problem is solved.

Fasting seems to get us into a position to receive more power from God, so we experience more miracles.

My personal observation tells me that most problems would be taken care of with three simple days of prayer and fasting. It's therapeutic mentally and emotionally.

In Moscow, a psychiatric unit had seven thousand patients afflicted with everything from schizophrenia to psychosis. Allen Cot, a doctor from America, went there to observe a "hunger experiment," which was essentially an exercise in fasting. They didn't feed those thousands of people anything but water for seven days, and at that time 87 percent of them were well enough to be released and sent home![5]

As leaders, we would do well to clear our minds and spirits of clutter by fasting.

PHYSICAL BENEFITS

Along with the spiritual and mental benefits, there are physical rewards that go with fasting. Luke 2:36-37 says:

> **And there was one Anna, a prophetess, the daughter of Phanuel, of the tribe of Aser: she was of a great age, and**

---

5   Cott, Allan, M.D., *Fasting: The Ultimate Diet*, p. 34-36, 1975, Bantam Books, New York, NY

> had lived with an husband seven years from her virgini-
> ty; And she *was* a widow of about fourscore and four
> years, which departed not from the temple, but served
> *God* with fastings and prayers night and day.

We don't know any more about this woman than what we find in these two verses. She was a prophetess. Her husband had died eighty-four years earlier. She was married seven years to her husband, so that makes ninety-one years. Let's suppose she was seventeen when she got married. That would make her 108 years of age. The average life span of a woman in that day was fifty to fifty-five years of age. So Anna outlived the average woman by a lifetime.

How?

What was the difference? The Bible mentions a couple of things. She served God with prayer. In this she was probably like most other good Jewish women. Second, she fasted much of the time. Could this be the secret to her spiritual effectiveness and even her longevity? I believe it's very possible.

I used to fast early in my ministry, but I stopped when things started to go well. I was encouraged to abandon fasting by a teaching that claimed: if Jesus is with us, we don't need to fast, based upon Matthew 9:15. I liked

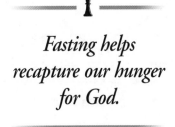

Fasting helps recapture our hunger for God.

that teaching! My appetite especially liked it. But after attending Loren Triplett's retirement banquet, I determined that I would return to fasting. Every year since then, my church has carried out a forty-day fast. Why? I want a deep hunger for

God. I want that spiritual clarity and focus. I want to be like the Annas, Elijahs, Pauls and Moseses of history. Don't you?

Anna lived twice as long as the average woman of that day. Is it possible you could double your life span with fasting? How about adding even fifteen extra years?

Dr. Otto Buckinger, founder of the European Buckinger Clinics, found astounding benefits from fasting as a therapy for his patients.[6] Cardiovascular and circulatory diseases reversed. Migraine headaches were cured as were glaucoma, digestive disorders, liver diseases, Crohn's disease, chronic colitis, ulcerative colitis, degenerative disease of the vertebral column, problems involving muscles and ligaments, skin diseases, allergies, psoriasis, eczema, respiratory diseases, bronchial asthma, chronic sinusitis, and psychosomatic disturbances including depression. Buckinger claims fasting detoxifies the body and is the fastest, safest, most effective known method of weight loss, healing, and longevity. Could it be that even the medical world is finding out that God was right?

Dr. Joel Furman, author of *Fasting and Eating for Your Health*, did a study at a New York animal clinic that made its animals fast two days a week. They lived twice as long as the animals that ate every day! Doctors believe it's because the body heals when given the opportunity.[7]

Even Benjamin Franklin said the best of all medicines are rest and fasting.

---

[6] Wilhelmi-Buchinger, Maria, *Fasting: The Buchinger Method,* p. 22, 1986, The C. W. Daniel Company, London, England UK

[7] Fuhrman, Joel M. D., 1995, St. Martin's Press, New York, NY

My greatgrandfather, Pa Dombrowski, was eighty-two when doctors told him he had cancer. The surgeons said if he didn't have surgery right away, he would die within three months. The Polish side of my family has a way with words, and Pa told the doctor to take this report and "shove it." He went back to the farm north of Lansing, Michigan, and fasted all dairy products, meats, and sweets. He started boiling rhubarb, and vegetables, and fruits. Three months later he was better than ever. A year later he was still out there plowing the fields. Sixteen years later, just before his ninety-ninth birthday, he died in his sleep. His heart stopped. They did an autopsy, and there was no cancer in him. Could it be that this miracle practice of fasting is meant to keep us healthy for long years of service to the Lord?

To see greater miracles and get through tough times, set yourself to fasting and praying.

You have a call and a destiny. God put you in a city, a township, a village, or a neighborhood for a purpose. But to see greater miracles and to get through tough spots, set yourself to fasting and praying. Let's be leaders like those in the first-century church. We can unleash miracles of all types by devoting ourselves to this proven lifestyle of fasting.

Next we'll look at another powerful character trait of emerging leaders: They know what they want!

POWER POINTS:

1. *When was the last time you fasted, and what were the results in your mind, body, and spirit?*

2. *What kinds of spiritual miracles and divine guidance do you need to receive about decisions you have to make as a leader? Would fasting help you in these areas? Explain.*

3. *When do you intend to fast next? For how long? What kind of fast will you undertake? Be specific and make a schedule.*

Editor's Note:

Order Dr. Dave Williams' best-selling book, "The Miracle Results of Fasting," by calling 1.800.888.7284 toll free. Also available at booksellers nationally.

As a leader in ministry, it should be easy to know what you want because you already know what God wants.

CHAPTER

EMERGING LEADERS KNOW WHAT THEY WANT

Once a year I teach a practical pastoral ministry class, and I give my students an assignment: they must list fifty things they want in the next ten years relating to life and ministry. To my continual surprise, the vast majority of students can't complete the assignment. They can't list fifty things they hope to gain or accomplish. They simply don't know what they want.

How can you fulfill the words of Jesus in Mark 11:24 without knowing what you want? That passage says:

> Therefore I say unto you, What things soever ye desire, when ye pray, believe that ye receive *them*, and ye shall have *them*.

Notice the words "what things soever ye *desire*." That means that before you pray, you have to know what you want!

People come to me all the time and say things like, "Pray that God will do something in my church."

I ask, "What do you want Him to do?" They respond, "I just want Him to move."

> *When our requests are in perfect harmony with what God wants, faith functions beautifully.*

What does that mean? Move next door? Move down the road? They have no idea.

People come to me and say, "Pray for me. The doctor gave me a bad report," or, "I'm drowning in debt. I need help." They tell me the problem but not the solution. When Bartimaeus was crying out, "Son of David, have mercy on me," Jesus asked, "What is it that you want?" (Mark 10:51) Jesus wanted Bartimaeus to be specific about the solution he wanted, not just about the problem. They know what they got but not what they want. I call this the Bartimaeus principle.

Some people ask me to pray that they'll have more money. I'm happy to pray for them if they know specifically how much more they want. But if they respond, as they usually do, "A little more than I have now," I feel like praying, "God, please give them more money," and then handing them a nickel and saying, "There, God answered your prayer — through me. Now you have a little more money."

The point is this: Emerging new church leaders *know what they want!*

Do you know what you want? Can you list fifty things you want in your life and ministry? You should have no problem at all. When our requests are in perfect harmony with what God wants, faith functions beautifully. The disciples knew precisely what they wanted, and in Acts 4 they asked God:

> And now, Lord, behold their threatenings: and grant unto thy servants, that with all boldness they may speak thy word, By stretching forth thine hand to heal; and that signs and wonders may be done by the name of thy holy child Jesus.

—Acts 4:29-30

That prayer probably took less than one minute, and within that time the earth began to shake. The Holy Spirit refilled them, and they went out and spoke the Word with fresh boldness, healing the sick, cleansing the lepers, opening blind eyes, performing signs and wonders, being delivered from jails, and having angelic intervention. They got specifically what they asked for. How did it start? They *knew* exactly what they wanted!

Before you pray you have to know what you want!

As a leader in ministry, it should be easy to know what you want because you already know what God wants. Does God want to heal? To bless? To promote and prosper? Does God want to save every person in your community? Yes, He does! You already know what He wants, so you should know what you want.

WHAT DO YOU KNOW?

Here's the mistake many leaders make: They want to figure out *how* before they determine *what*. For example, I didn't know how to be a pastor when I started, and some say I still don't. I still feel like a rookie even today after twenty-seven years, but I can say this: I know what I want. When God pointed me to Acts 13:44, that became a theme for my ministry in Lansing:

> And the next sabbath day came almost the whole city together to hear the word of God.

I remember thinking, "Is it really possible that the whole city could come together to hear the Word of God?" That became *what* I wanted.

Notice I said "what" not "how." I didn't know *how* to bring that verse about, but I knew *what* I wanted.

In 1983 I was fasting and praying, sprawled out on the floor with my Bible, a pencil and paper, and the Holy Spirit said, "I want you to build a healing center and call it Gilead, the place of another chance." Gilead in the Bible was a city of refuge, a place of safety. It was also where David trained his captains. The Lord said to my heart, "Gilead Healing Center will be a place of healing and of another chance, where people will be trained to flow in spiritual gifts to heal the sick, cleanse the lepers, and open blind eyes." I agreed, "Okay, Lord, I'll do it," but I didn't know how. I had no idea when or how; I just knew *what*. So since 1983, I've been praying about the *what*. In God's time it all came to pass, and in June 2003 we dedicated Gilead Healing Center, a multimillion dollar project debt-free to the glory of God.

You don't have to immediately know "how;" you just need to know "what" you want!

Don't be like a hunter firing aimlessly into the woods, hoping to hit something. Don't just take what life gives you. Emerging twenty-first-century leaders write down *specifically* what they want in their ministries and in their churches in harmony with God's will. They are not like the Beatles' "Nowhere Man," "sitting in his nowhere land making all his nowhere plans for nobody. He doesn't have a point of view and knows not where he's going to. Isn't he a bit like you and me?" I hope not!

You don't have to know how; you just need to know what.

How To Get ANYTHING You Want

God actually gives us principles in the Bible for getting what we desire. Jesus said, "All things *are* possible to him that believeth" (Mark 9:23). Later He said:

> Verily I say unto you, If ye have faith, and doubt not, ye shall not only do this *which is done* to the fig tree, but also if ye shall say unto this mountain, Be thou removed, and be thou cast into the sea; it shall be done. And all things, whatsoever ye shall ask in prayer, believing, ye shall receive.
>
> —Matthew 21:21-22

How do we move from knowing what we want to seeing those things come to pass? Jesus gave His disciples a simple five-point plan.

■ 1. HAVE FAITH!

Faith is a spiritual force, the substance of things hoped for and the evidence of things we don't yet see (Hebrews 11:1). A person sick in body may receive prayer for healing and see no evidence that the prayer worked. But faith brings the answer from the realm of God's infinite power.

■ 2. DON'T DOUBT!

Doubt involves the mind, just as faith springs from the spirit. Many times I have stood in faith on God's Word, believing for a promise, only to hear teaching that tells my mind I should not believe it. That's when doubt can arise, but doubt is a pernicious enemy of faith.

It's actually dangerous to doubt God's original word to you. A prophet in the Old Testament received direction from God to travel to Israel and back taking a certain route and fasting the whole time (I Kings 13:9). He went to Israel, delivered his prophetic message to the king, but on his way home, an old prophet sidetracked him and induced him to disobey God's word. He ate dinner with the old prophet and didn't go straight home. When continuing on his way home, a lion killed the young prophet because he had doubted the first word and, subsequently, disobeyed.

> *It's actually dangerous to doubt God's word to you.*

Don't entertain doubt, even when it seems to come from a credible source. Paul said, "I conferred not with flesh and blood" (Galatians 1:16). He didn't want to give doubt a foothold.

One time early in our marriage, my wife Mary Jo and I needed money. We decided to stand on the promise of Mark 10:29-30 where God said:

> And Jesus answered and said, Verily I say unto you, There is no man that hath left house, or brethren, or sisters, or father, or mother, or wife, or children, or lands, for my sake, and the gospel's, but he shall receive an hundredfold now in this time, houses, and brethren, and sisters, and mothers, and children, and lands, with persecutions; and in the world to come eternal life.

Our bills were mounting so we went through the couch cushions and old piggy banks looking for money, and we scraped up $8.00! We had $800 worth of bills to pay. I said, "Lord, here is our $8.00. It won't put a dent in these bills, so we give this to You believing Your promise to multiply it back a hundred times over."

The next day I got a newsletter in the mail from a preacher, and the lead article was titled "The Hundred-fold Heresy." I made the mistake of reading the article, and my mind was battered with doubt.

Mary Jo and I took a walk around the neighborhood and prayed about it. Later that evening as we praised and waited on the Lord, the Holy Spirit gave us a word: "I say unto you, My children, all Scripture is given by inspiration of God and is profitable for doctrine" (II Timothy 3:16). We accepted that as confirmation, and my doubts were banished. The next day I got a telephone call that ultimately brought me $880! God had multiplied that little offering more than a hundred-fold.

■ **3. SPEAK TO THE MOUNTAIN.**

Jesus never said to speak *about* the mountain but speak *to* the mountain. If that mountain is a sickness, you speak to the sickness. You don't speak about how big and terrible it looks. David spoke *to* Goliath, while everybody else was speaking *about* Goliath and growing more terrified.

I know a man in Florida who bought a motel that was hemorrhaging money. For a while this man spoke *about* the problem with the motel, but he soon realized that wasn't doing any good, so one morning he changed tactics. He walked outside, pointed at his motel, and yelled, "In the name of Jesus, mountain of red ink, I command you to go. Motel, I command you to start making money for me!"

> *Get a tenacious grip on what you're believing for.*

That might sound stupid, but on one occasion Jesus spoke to a tree! And don't we all speak to inanimate objects, like our cars or street lights? "I'm in a hurry; don't turn red!" "Come on, Betsy, start!" I tell you the truth, within three months that motel was profitable and running in the black.

■ **4. ASK IN PRAYER BELIEVING.**

In John 16:23-24 Jesus said:

> And in that day ye shall ask me nothing. Verily, verily, I say unto you, Whatsoever ye shall ask the Father in my name, he will give *it* you.
>
> Hitherto have ye asked nothing in my name: ask, and ye shall receive, that your joy may be full.

■ **5. RECEIVE!**

In the Greek that means seize, accept, and forcefully take. Why do we have to forcefully take it? Because the devil opposes everything you want to pull out of that invisible realm of supply. Why do churches have so much trouble when they go into a building program or a new evangelism effort? They face demonic resistance. As a leader, you must teach people to receive forcefully, not passively. You must make the vision real to them so their minds and hearts grasp it and won't let go. Get a tenacious grip on what you're believing for. That's how to receive.

Don't entertain doubt, even if from a credible source.

Do you know what you want? Can you list fifty things right here and now that you want in your life and ministry in the next ten years? If not, dwell on this for a while. Stir up the vision God has put inside of you. Emerging leaders know what they want and go after it with every expectation of succeeding.

That is *our* job in these last days. If we don't know what we want, how will the people we lead know? And if we don't lead forcefully and with great joy in the coming years, who will?

POWER POINT:

1. *List fifty things you want in your life and ministry in the next ten years.*

2. *Has God given you answers on how to accomplish any of the above? Explain.*

3. *Do the people you are leading know what you want? Ask a few of them. If they can't state it clearly and immediately, make a plan so that every person you lead will know exactly what you want.*

Emerging leaders aren't looking
for somebody else to walk in
with a silver platter of success
and hand it to them.

CHAPTER

EMERGING LEADERS ACCEPT RESPONSIBILITY

I went to my dentist recently, and the hygienist, an acquaintance of mine, came in and greeted me. I asked her, "What's happening?"

She whined, "I'm still working here. I figured I'd be retired and wealthy by now."

I responded kindly, "You should have planned it that way."

She groaned, "I thought my husband was going to make it happen for us."

That passing comment is revealing, and as leaders we

should take it to heart. Some people spend their lifetime waiting for somebody else to "make it happen."

Have you noticed how some people's lives never change? They're the same today as they were fifteen or twenty years ago — just a little older and grayer. They seem to spend decades waiting on God or waiting on other people to accomplish their dreams. They don't actively use what they've been given. They blame others for their stagnation just as Adam blamed Eve and Eve blamed the serpent for their sin.

When you know what you want and that desire builds up in you, you will develop this next characteristic of the emerging twenty-first-century leaders. *You'll accept responsibility for the success in your life, work, and ministry.*

> *Happiness is your responsibility and yours alone, and you'll never be happy unless you fulfill your calling.*

Emerging leaders aren't looking for somebody else to walk in with a silver platter of success and hand it to them. They realize they have everything they need to accomplish what God has called them to accomplish. They have the Word of God, the ministry of prayer, the ministry of fasting, and the same kind of angels around them that other believers have. They have the same Blood of Jesus and the same Holy Spirit. They have all the tools and heavenly support they need right at their fingertips.

Emerging twenty-first-century leaders know this fundamental principle of life: *"I am responsible for my own life. I am responsible for my own ministry. I am responsible for my thoughts. I am responsible for my words. I am responsible for my actions. I am responsible for my happiness."*

HAPPINESS

People who are always looking to somebody else to make them happy will never become authentic twenty-first-century leaders. Your husband or wife will never make you happy. (You probably knew that already!) Happiness is your responsibility and yours alone, and you'll never be happy unless you're fulfilling your calling. Jesus gave *you* the calling. He gave *you* the mandate and the authority. He commanded:

> Go ye into all the world, and preach the gospel to every creature. He that believeth and is baptized shall be saved; but he that believeth not shall be damned.

> —Mark 16:15-16

The idea is, "You do it!" And the disciples did. They went everywhere, the Lord working with them confirming the Word with signs following. They took one step, and the Holy Spirit propelled them through the next ninety-nine!

People say, "Look at all that man of God has accomplished." It wasn't him at all; he just took one step, and the Holy Spirit catapulted him over ninety-nine more.

A little boy played on the same basketball team with his older brother in a neighborhood game. The big brother made a hundred points, and the little brother didn't make any. At the end of the game, he looked up at his big brother and said, "Boy, we sure beat 'em, didn't we?" That's how we are with Jesus. He scored a hundred for you and for me. You may not feel like you've even made a basket in the game of life, but Jesus scored plenty of points, and you're part of His team. That makes you a winner.

I used to blame my wife, in a lighthearted manner, about my weight change. On our wedding day, I weighed 143 pounds. Now I weigh at least forty more pounds than that. I would tell people, "I used to weigh 143 pounds; then I got married and look at me now." I was shifting the blame off myself and on to my wife! That wasn't very kind, and it wasn't even accurate — it was my fault, not hers — so I quit saying it.

But many would-be leaders rely on excuses throughout their sorry careers. They blame their congregations, the district, the big church in town, the little church in town, the other preacher in town, and the televangelist. In truth, excuse-givers will never be a part of the emerging twenty-first-century leaders because they're filled with blame. I know a former pastor who is on the scrap heap of life today. Four different churches failed under his leadership, but somehow it was never his fault. It was the "occultic Masons" who founded his community, and so there was too much spiritual battle going on. Or the people in the church didn't want to seek first the Kingdom of God, in his view. Then surprisingly, another pastor replaced him, and the church grew and prospered. Was the problem with the church? The people? The history of the town? No, it was the pastor. He never took responsibility.

The Blood of Jesus has never cleansed an excuse, but it has cleansed plenty of sin. Excuse-making is sin — we need to confess it.

> If we confess our sins, he is faithful and just to forgive us *our* sins, and to cleanse us from all unrighteousness.

> —1 John 1:9

CALLING ALL RESPONSIBLE LEADERS

When I first started pastoring in Lansing, Michigan, spiritual people told me there would never be a great church here. A man who prophesied all the time said, "Brother, I know you have big ideas and dreams, but this is Lansing. God has shown me that Lansing has a Samson spirit that quenches His work anytime there is a revival." I'd never heard of the Samson spirit, so I didn't pay much attention to that.

Next, an intellectual man came up to me and said, "Reverend Williams, in my studies I see that we are in the post-Christian era, so we really can't expect the same kind of results that the first-century believers had."

Excuse-givers will never be a part of the emerging twenty-first-century leaders because they are filled with blame.

Then, another "prophet" told me we couldn't have a great church in Lansing because Lansing is the seat of political influence in Michigan, and there are too many political demons.

Somebody else said, "I hear you're trusting God for big things. Just don't get into the numbers game. Some of these pastors are only interested in quantity, not quality. At my church we go for quality, and that's what pleases God." I asked, "How many quality people do you have in your church?" She answered, "Twenty-three, but we're building quality into them." I got to thinking; if you are really building quality, you'll get quantity, because quality attracts quantity.

Excuse-making is a sin – we need to confess it.

All these "prophetic" suggestions might sound logical or spiritual, in their way, but I knew my calling wasn't based on man's ideas or theories. By most standards I shouldn't even be a pastor. I was not educated as a pastor. I'd spent four years studying engineering in the U.S. Navy, engineering in college, and six years at the Board of Water and Light electrical department doing everything from working the boilers to running control boards to drawing blueprints and schematics for training manuals. Logically, perhaps, I should have failed as a pastor. But I knew I had the same Holy Spirit, the same Bible, the same study tools that are available to anyone.

Early in my ministry I preached a series, "A Great Vision For Our Great Church." Ninety-eight people came for the first message. Thirteen weeks later, there were over three hundred people attending. What if I'd heeded the advice of the "experts" who told me not to dream big? We might still be at ninety-eight people. Today we have over 12,000 members in Lansing and in our twenty-nine satellite churches.

Everything must be discerned according to the Word of God. Ultimately, leaders of the twenty-first century will accept responsibility for their own success. Think of the responsibility Jesus accepted. He was in all points tempted like you and me, and yet He had to stay sinless, or the whole plan would have fallen through. He didn't make excuses. He accepted responsibility for your sake and mine.

Today God put you and me in big cities, little communities, villages, and towns to accept responsibility for the sake of others who will one day be saved, filled with the Holy Spirit, and preaching the marvelous Good News of Jesus. That is our job, and nobody else is responsible for it but us.

I remember a young man named Josh, a high schooler in Maple Valley, who was a member of our church for a number of years. He developed a heart for the school football team on which he played. One morning at 3 a.m., God woke him up and said, "Will you accept responsibility for their souls?"

If you are building quality, you'll get quantity, because quality attracts quantity.

Josh trembled as he said, "Yes Lord." He interceded for three hours that night, naming each member of that football team. He knew what God wanted, and he was ready to take responsibility.

After football practice that night, he gathered all the guys in the locker room and said, "I'm really scared. I don't even know the right way to do this. But last night the Lord woke me up and asked me to take responsibility for your souls." He shared the Gospel with the team and asked them to receive Jesus. The Holy Spirit came down in that locker room, and all those tough football players were weeping like babies. One by one, Josh led them in the prayer of salvation. He went home, his head spinning with what happened.

You will get powerful results when you accept responsibility for your church, neighborhood, and city.

The next night Josh was walking home, and a popular girl that hardly ever paid any attention to him drove by, stopped, and said, "I heard something happened in the locker room last night, and I really need to know about it. Let me give you a ride home." So Josh hopped in her car and shared the Gospel with her. She was in tears by the time they pulled up to his house. Josh led her in the prayer of salvation. She was the sister of a football player who was sick the day before and had not been in the locker room the night the team accepted Jesus. She went home and led her brother to the Lord.

You will get powerful results when you accept responsibility for your church, neighborhood, and city, like Josh accepted responsibility for his football team. I encourage you to be like Josh instead of like that pastor I knew who constantly blamed others for his failure. Will you be an effective twenty-first-century leader? Then annihilate the excuses! Put your hand to the plow, and look straight at the goal — taking responsibility the entire way.

POWER POINTS:

1. *Think of an incident where you took responsibility even though it meant taking blame. What did you learn? Did you grow out of that experience? Explain.*

2. *Rate yourself on a scale of 1-10. Do you take responsibility immediately and fully for everything that happens in your life (10), or do you try to shirk responsibility (1)?*

    1   2   3   4   5   6   7   8   9   10

3. *Write a short prayer asking God to point out areas in which you need to accept more responsibility. Perhaps you need to take responsibility for the salvation of your city or for the mending of a relationship or for a circumstance that has arisen at your place of work. Whatever it is, ask God to point it out so you can take responsibility for it.*

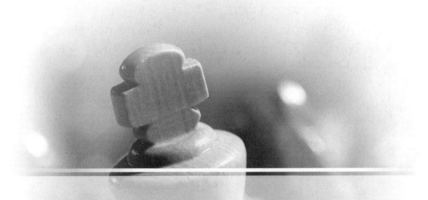

Distraction brings loss,
missed opportunities,
and wasted years.

CHAPTER

EMERGING LEADERS AVOID DISTRACTIONS

As a pastor or leader, you often have a different schedule than the rest of the world. On Saturdays, while others are out boating or fishing or just lying around the house, a pastor is usually praying and polishing his Sunday sermon.

I spend Saturdays praying and staying in the Word as much as I can because I want to be genuinely anointed for Sunday morning services. I don't go to basketball games or out for coffee or golfing on Saturdays. Nonetheless, sometimes when I'm praying I'll notice something small, perhaps a cupboard door open in my home office. It starts distracting me, so I walk over to close it. But while I'm closing it, I notice there's coffee in the cupboard, and I realize I haven't made coffee yet. I start making a pot, and while it's brewing I think, "I may as well look at my e-mail while I'm waiting. Maybe I should check my voice mail messages too." And before I realize what's happening, I'm tapping on my desk and listening to my phone messages. I've gone from having an intimate conversation with the Father to checking my voice mail!

Distractions are everywhere. They interrupt our prayer time, our work time, corporate worship times — anytime.

One Sunday morning the congregation was worshiping God, and I opened my eyes a moment and saw an exit light blinking. The bulb was apparently defective. That was enough to jerk me away from my posture of worship. I was so distracted that I couldn't get my mind back on the Lord, so I called a maintenance man to fix the bulb!

The devil uses distractions to get our lives out of focus. In Luke 9, Jesus was wrapping up a conversation with some people who were giving excuses as to why they couldn't answer God's call. He said:

> No man, having put his hand to the plough, and looking back, is fit for the kingdom of God.
>
> —Luke 9:62

The Living Bible puts it this way:

> Anyone who lets himself be distracted from the work I plan for him is not fit for the Kingdom of God.

Imagine the tragedy of not being fit to receive the blessings, secrets, mysteries, benefits, and advantages of the Kingdom of God.

Deuteronomy 28 says a similar thing. God was pronouncing blessings on people who listened to and obeyed His voice and curses for those who didn't. Then He came to verse 14 and said:

> And thou shalt not go aside from any of the words which I command thee this day, *to* the right hand, or *to* the left, to go after other gods to serve them.
>
> —Deuteronomy 28:14

He was saying in essence, "I have laid out the plan for you; *don't get distracted.* Stay on track."

Picture yourself in an NBA basketball game, and your team is down by one point. There are three seconds to go, and you've just been fouled. You now have the opportunity to be either a champ or a chump. You step up to the foul line for your two free throws. Half the people in the arena don't want you to make a basket, so they're yelling and waving flags and trying to distract you as best they can. The ball misses a little bit and rolls around the rim and onto the floor. As you step up to that foul line, you could say, "Referee, would you

♟

Distractions interrupt our prayer time, our work time, corporate worship times – any time.

please have everybody be quiet? I need to focus." He's not going to do it. He can't control the crowd.

That's the way it is in life. The devil seeks to distract us from the greatest things God wants to do through us. He is a master of distractions, waving anything he can in our faces at a time when we need to perform. We can't make him sit down and shut up, but we can train ourselves to not be distracted.

AVIATE, NAVIGATE, COMMUNICATE

Satan knows that to defeat and destroy you, he first has to distract you. He distracted Adam and Eve by showing them the beautiful fruit (Genesis 3). He tried to distract Jesus by showing Him the kingdoms of the world:

> **Again, the devil taketh him up into an exceeding high mountain, and sheweth him all the kingdoms of the world, and the glory of them;**
>
> **And saith unto him, All these things will I give thee, if thou wilt fall down and worship me.**
>
> —Matthew 4:8-9

A distraction is:

- Anything that takes your focus off what you are supposed to be doing.

- Anything that gets you to turn aside from God's commands, God's plans, or God's Word.

If you are a leader, distractions are particularly harmful because they not only affect you but also the people you're leading. If you're too distracted to put together an anointed, well-prepared sermon, for example, your people will suffer. If you are too distracted to cultivate and communicate a big vision, your people will not know what to do or where they fit in.

In the Bible we're told that the priests needed seven solid days of focus before they were ready for the anointing. I don't know how ministers expect to have a full anointing without focusing on the Lord for several days. I don't know how some can pray a three-minute prayer and think they'll have spiritual power. We're told in Jeremiah 7:24 that the priests lost their focus, became distracted and concerned with nonsense, and went backward instead of forward.

> *Anything that pulls you away from your calling is a distraction.*

> But they hearkened not, nor inclined their ear, but walked in the counsels *and* in the imagination of their evil heart, and went backward, and not forward.

> —Jeremiah 7:24

Distractions cause our lives to go backward instead of forward. Backward spiritually. Backward intellectually. Backward financially. Backward in our business, our ministry, our families, and our relationships.

It's never good to go backward. The Kingdom of God advances, and so must we!

When I was attending flight school, I had to take a flight check ride with an FAA representative to prove that I could pilot an airplane. During that flight he did everything he could to distract me, to see if I could maintain my priorities in the cockpit. He secretly turned off my radio, changed dials, and created one distraction after another. The idea was to test and reinforce my priorities when flying. Those priorities are, in order:

- **1. AVIATE**

- **2. NAVIGATE**

- **3. COMMUNICATE**[8]

You must follow the priorities in proper order. If you are in a tailspin, you don't want to get on your radio and say, "Hello tower, I'm in a spin. Where's the nearest airport?" No, you want to aviate. You want to pull the plane out of that spin. You don't even care about navigating at this point; you just don't want to hit the ground.

On the night of December 29, 1972, Eastern Airlines Flight 401 took off from New York and headed toward Miami, Florida. Less than three hours later, the aircraft reached Florida.[9] Unfortunately it did so as a scattered wreck over the marshes of the Florida Everglades. One hundred and one lives were instantly thrust into eternity.[10]

What went wrong?

On initial approach the pilots noticed that a little 89-cent indicator light was out. They had the plane, filled with passengers, in autopilot while they fiddled around with the light. They could have landed, and maintenance people could have taken care of it, but the pilot and copilot got distracted trying to change the lightbulb and didn't realize one of them had hit

---

8 Hayenga, Daniel, "Aviate, navigate, communicate", *Flying Safety*, July, 2002

9 Bartelski, Jan, "Disasters in the Air: Mysterious Air Disasters Explained, *Airlife Publishing*, England, 2001

10 Shear, Barry, "Crash of Flight 401", *Delta Library Company*, 1978, England

the control yoke and knocked the autopilot off. They crashed in the Everglades killing almost everyone on board.

A little distraction can make a big difference. Distraction brings loss, missed opportunities, and wasted years.

Two voices are always calling for our attention; the voice of wisdom and the voice of stupidity. Proverbs 5:10 says certain distractions will cause strangers to benefit from our work. Proverbs 8:5 says wisdom calls out to all who are gullible and lack common sense, "Come." Then several verses later it says similarly that stupidity calls out to all who are gullible and lack common sense (9:16). Lady Stupidity wants to distract us. She tempts us by saying, "Let's have our fill of fun," but she leads to laziness and poverty. After a while you fall headfirst and end up on the scrap heap of life.

> *Hell is populated with those who got distracted from their main purpose.*

Wisdom calls. Stupidity calls. Only we can decide which call we will respond to. There are always other voices calling out, "Take this road, stop for a while, take it easy," and the Bible makes it clear that those roads go nowhere except to failure. They are distractions.

A STRONG MAN'S DISTRACTIONS

What are the distractions for a leader? The possibilities are endless. They could be pleasure, power, fame, leisure, sports, golf, television, unhealthy hair-splitting theological arguments, food, video games, books, magazines. Anything that pulls you away from your calling, anointing, and God's priorities is a distraction.

Distractions can devastate a life forever. Samson was distracted from his honorable calling to be Israel's deliverer. He sat around drinking with God's enemies, exchanging riddles and rhymes, and going crazy over a "hot" lady who had no regard for God. He told his parents, "I want to marry that girl. She's hot!" They scolded, "Samson, you're a Nazarite; you've taken a vow. You're supposed to represent God and be Israel's deliverer. Why are you looking at ungodly women?" And he said, "I don't care about that now, Mom and Dad — I want her."

Distractions are harmful because they not only affect you but also the people you're leading.

So he became engaged to her. And, predictibly she betrayed him by sharing his secrets with his enemies. Samson, in anger over her betrayal, called her an old cow and booted her out. You'd think he would have learned, but later on he did it again, this time with a woman named Delilah who also betrayed him and gave the secret of his strength to his enemies. They captured him and gouged out his eyes. He would never see again. He became a blind slave under the dictatorship of his enemies the rest of his life all because he allowed himself to become distracted from God's priorities (See Judges 16).

Worse yet, distractions can keep people from going to Heaven. Jesus told us there is only one way to get to Heaven and that is through Him (John 14:6). If you follow a religious system, a philosophy that does not have Jesus Christ as the only Savior and Lord, you're going to hell. It's that simple. Hell is populated with those on the road of stupidity who got distracted from the main purpose of life. The fear of the Lord is the beginning of wisdom (Proverbs 1:7). It's hard to distract someone who reveres the Lord and honors His Word.

The new breed of leaders — emerging leaders — are aware of and shun all distractions. They put blinders on so they won't go to the right or left. They stay on the straight and true path that leads to the fulfillment of their calling.

Be a powerful twenty-first-century emerging leader.

Next we'll explore this topic of distractions and talk about how to avoid them.

POWER POINTS:

1. *What are your biggest distractions? Name them.*

2. *How do you avoid distractions? Does your strategy work well, or does it need retooling?*

3. *How can you better avoid distractions in the future? Be specific about what you will do when faced with a distraction.*

We get distracted when we trust our natural eyes more than the eyes of our heart.

CHAPTER

WHAT CAUSES DISTRACTIONS?

There are several basic reasons leaders become distracted.

We get distracted when we trust our natural eyes more than the eyes of our heart. I preached a message once called, "The Way Things Look Are Not Necessarily The Way Things Are." That has never been more true, and yet many people cancel out their prayers with immediate unbelief because it doesn't *look* like anything has happened. They conclude very quickly, "God didn't do anything," and in the spirit realm, their prayer is cancelled.

A harrowing story illustrates this in the life of King Saul. It's a stern warning to us as leaders.

God told Samuel the prophet to instruct Saul not to go to war for seven days. At the end of seven days, Samuel the prophet was to make a sacrifice, and God would then grant Isreal victory over the Philistines.

Saul started out well. He prepared for war by building his army, but when they *looked* at the Philistines and their weapons, the Israelites became scared. Some of them jumped down wells to hide; others went across the river; others went completely AWOL and were never seen again. Saul's army seemed to be deteriorating by the minute — or at least *that's how it looked* in the natural. But Saul said, "I'm going to trust God," so he waited the seven days as instructed. As the end of that time approached, Samuel hadn't arrived yet to make the necessary sacrifice. Saul became especially nervous, and instead of waiting for Samuel, he made the sacrifice to God on his own. That was not what God had ordered. Saul had caved in to the distractions. Not long after that, Samuel arrived and said, "Saul what have you done?" Saul made excuses. "You didn't arrive on time, and I got worried. My army was falling apart, and I knew if I didn't make the sacrifice, I wouldn't have the favor of God, so I went ahead and did it." Samuel responded with these chilling words:

We can get distracted when we have the wrong kind of friends.

> Thou hast done foolishly: thou hast not kept the commandment of the LORD thy God, which he commanded thee: for now would the LORD have established thy kingdom upon Israel for ever.

> But now thy kingdom shall not continue: the LORD hath
> sought him a man after his own heart, and the LORD hath
> commanded him *to be* captain over his people, because
> thou hast not kept *that* which the LORD commanded
> thee.
>
> —I Samuel 13:13-14

Saul believed what he *saw* in the natural and acted on it
rather than waiting on the word of the Lord. We make the
same kinds of mistakes when we are distracted by what *appears*
to be true. In fact, we are to "walk by faith, not by sight"
(II Corinthians 5:7). As it turned out for Saul, the Philistines
never invaded. He gave up his anointing and kingdom out of
fear of something that *never happened.* That's what distractions
do to leaders. They can take our eyes off the priorities; they
prod us to disobey, thinking that we're doing something good.

Distracted By Desires And The Wrong Crowd

We can also get distracted when our personal desires
become dominant once again. Samson is a good example. His
strong desire for silly distractions cost him his vision, his free-
dom, and eventually his life. You cannot focus on the will of
God and conflicting desires at the same time. In Mark 4:18-19,
Jesus gave the parable of the sower.

> And these are they which are sown among thorns; such as
> hear the word, And the cares of this world, and the deceit-
> fulness of riches, and the lusts of other things entering in,
> choke the word, and it becometh unfruitful.

Jesus tells us those thorns were the desire for other things,
the deceitfulness of riches, and the cares of this life. The only

things that can choke out God's supernatural promises are distractions like these. If we desire something else and worry about the cares of this life, it distracts us from the prize. It takes us off course.

We also get distracted when we have the wrong kind of friends. Proverbs 13:20 says, "He that walketh with wise men shall be wise: but a companion of fools shall be destroyed." In Psalm 80, Israel cried out to God for deliverance saying in essence, "We've messed up, but please restore us." How did they mess up? They made ungodly alliances with people who didn't serve God. Instead of influencing those people for God, their own hearts were corrupted. They were eventually captured and taken into slavery. Why? Because they were distracted from what was really important — God's purposes.

> *The habit of reading your Bible will become a strong bulwark against distractions.*

Leaders in previous generations have spent an incredible amount of time putting out proverbial brush fires. Every urgent situation distracted them from their vision and purpose.

This is not true of the new breed of emerging leaders. They focus; they stay on target with their calling and with the important key matters in life and ministry.

Pastors, for example, often receive unsigned "sniper notes." You know the kind. "I love you, pastor, but .... God has shown me ..." They are distractions from the enemy. The word "occult" actually means "secret." And anyone who sends a secret note, whether it's a so-called prophecy, word from the Lord, or personal opinion, is not walking in the light, but darkness. They are pawns of the devil, yet believe themselves to be God's favorites. Distractions.

There seems to be a satanic, conspiratorial effort to shift a leader's focus from the things that are most important to God's heart. Perhaps it's a letter arriving every week, signed or unsigned, pointing out something the leader said or did wrong. Distractions.

Relational problems can be a source of distraction also. A local pastor used to call my secretary to set up appointments with me. He came to my office and wanted to argue over a host of peripheral, non-essential issues. He called his Bible, "my sword for fighting." It got to be a ridiculous waste of time, so I told my secretary that I would accept no more appointments with this man.

So he tried a different tactic. He called my office and demanded, "I need to make an appointment with Pastor Williams."

My secretary responded, "I'm sorry, Pastor Williams is not taking appointments right now."

"Well, he better meet with me because if he doesn't he'll be violating the Scriptures of Matthew 18:15-17 which says:

> Moreover if thy brother shall trespass against thee, go and tell him his fault between thee and him alone: if he shall hear thee, thou hast gained thy brother.

> But if he will not hear thee, then take with thee one or
> two more, that in the mouth of two or three witnesses
> every word may be established. And if he shall neglect
> to hear them, tell it unto the church: but if he neglect to
> hear the church, let him be unto thee as an heathen man
> and a publican.

"And I need to come and tell him his fault between him and me alone."

"Oh, well, in that case, I'll check with Pastor Williams and get back with you," my secretary assured him, knowing that I would never deliberately violate God's instructions.

When she told me, it was like having a monkey on my back. On one hand I didn't want to meet with this negative, whinny, know-it-all. On the other hand, I didn't want to violate Scripture. So I prayed and researched the matter and made a liberating discovery. The Hebrews understood this completely. The disciples understood it too. When Jesus said, "if thy *brother* shall trespass against thee," He was speaking about those who were part of the same "brotherhood." In other words, members of the same church or fellowship. He was *not* speaking about everyone who calls himself a "brother."

Often when members leave a church in anger, they will later want to set up an appointment with the pastor to whine and drone on and on about how "somebody done me wrong." Since they have voluntarily removed themselves from fellowship, a pastor has no obligation to meet with them, accept their input, or listen to their endless complaints.

The new breed of emerging leaders focuses on building disciples, not repairing the willfully dysfunctional and disobedient. They spend 98% of their time on the 98% of the people who are committed and ready to move ahead with God. They'll give perhaps 2% to the whiners, quitters, and rebels, but no more. They know when enough is enough.

Now back to the pastor who wanted an appointment. My secretary called him back and told him that I'd meet with him no more. He made his threats, gave his warnings, and hung up. That's the last I heard of him.

Stifled leaders take on other people's "monkeys." The emerging leaders don't. They stay focused. They are kind to problematic people but refuse to accept man-made burdens.

For example, suppose a minister from another city is being forced to resign from his church. He has taken the church from 150 in attendance down to 70 because of his annoying personality and the arrogant way he treats people. He comes to tell you his problem and expects you to go to his board to stand up for him.

An emerging leader won't accept the responsibility to "save" that pastor's ministry unless the Lord specifically moves on his heart to do so. The emerging leader is not unkind but moves by God's voice and God's Word only — not what others think he should be moved by.

Some people come to you and try to unload all their problems on your back, so-to-speak, expecting you to do something about it. Some leaders will accept that burden — that "monkey" — and spend countless precious hours away from their own priorities to try to solve the other person's self-induced problems. Not the emerging leader.

There are carnal people, used by the devil, who come and dump their load on you. They...

... Expect you to find them a spouse.

... Expect you to attend everything they think is important.

... Expect you to read any book they dump on you.

... Expect you to listen to any tape they give you.

... Expect you to interpret their dreams.

... Expect you to be available every time they call.

... Expect you to be their all-in-all.

... Expect you to find them a job.

... Expect you to give them a hand out.

... Expect you to pay their bills.

The list goes on into infinity.

The emerging leaders are not distracted by what they are *not* called to engage in. Instead, they stay resolute in their uncompromising focus on that which they *are* called to focus.

The emerging leader accepts responsibility for his own life, work, decisions, and actions and knows that you can never really help anyone who won't accept responsibility for their own situation.

Distractions. They're everywhere.

How do we avoid distractions? Let me give you some hints.

DITCHING DISTRACTIONS

■ CHOOSE WISDOM AND NOT STUPIDITY.

This choosing is not something passive. If we don't choose wisdom, stupidity will choose us! Stupidity can pose as wise arguments. Many Christians spend inordinate amounts of time arguing about nonessential matters. Arguments of any kind, which stray from the basic Gospel, can become distractions.

■ PRAY EVERY DAY.

Pray that you'll possess the wisdom to stay on target with your life and work. Set aside fifteen minutes or more, and get quiet before the Lord. Ministers ought to pray at least an hour — preferably two — every day to nurture their anointing. We should pray without ceasing throughout the day, but there needs to also be that daily special quiet time before the Lord. Praying and staying in His presence helps us fulfill the biblical command that says:

> Casting down imaginations, and every high thing that exalteth itself against the knowledge of God, and bringing into captivity every thought to the obedience of Christ.
>
> —2 Corinthians 10:5

■ READ AND MEDITATE ON GOD'S WORD.

Read one or two chapters every day. Even if you get up late, read at least one verse, but do it every day consistently. The habit will become a strong bulwark against distractions. Besides your regular reading, you'd also do well to read a chapter of Proverbs every day.

■ **RETURN TO THE BASICS.**

Life becomes incredibly complicated if you don't practice pruning. Sometimes the things that are supposed to help us actually hinder us. A man sold a new computer system to a business owner and three months later asked him how his business was doing. "Bankrupt," the owner replied. "I'm spending all day maintaining the computer system and I'm not out there with my customers." At some point we have to get back to basics.

■ **TAKE A REST.**

We'll talk about this more in chapter nine. In Matthew 8:24 Jesus was sleeping. If Jesus needed a rest, you need a rest too. If God rested after six days of creation, you need a rest too.

A chef friend of mine opened a classy deli-style restaurant by the local shopping mall. He went in early to design the menu and cook the meals. The business grew greater than he had originally imagined because of the blessing of the Lord. He needed to come up with a new spring menu but couldn't think of anything. He worked nonstop trying to come up with ideas, but his creative mind became like a dry creek bed. He came to church on a Sunday night when I talked about the importance of rest. The next day he decided, "I'm not going to work today. Somebody else can cook the food. I'm just going to stay home and rest." He rested and got a good night's sleep. He refused to wonder how things were going. When he woke up on Tuesday morning, it was as though an angel came into his

> *Pray that you will possess the wisdom to stay on target.*

room and handed him the new spring menu. He wrote out the ideas. On top of that, when he checked the figures for the day before, the net income was up in spite of his absence!

Even when you feel like you can't afford a rest, do it anyway.

God blesses you when you obey Him. There are a million excuses to not rest, not pray, not read the Bible, but don't believe one of them. Stick to the plan, and it will help you avoid distractions.

The new breed, emerging twenty-first-century leaders, avoid distractions and stay on target with their call and anointing.

Next we'll talk about managing the unique stress that comes with a leadership position.

POWER POINTS:

1. *Do you have a daily routine of prayer and Bible reading? What is it? Explain.*

2. *Do you need to return to the basics of life and cut off extraneous activities? Which activities are taking up time but not producing fruit? Explain.*

3. *Do you need a vacation? Are distractions more appealing because you're worn out? Ask your spouse or someone close to you to give their opinion about whether you need a break. Create a plan for regular breaks.*

*All leaders face inner stresses
that are caused by the outer
pressures of life.*

CHAPTER 8

DISTRESS SIGNALS IN LEADERSHIP

You know how it is: When everything is going well, the leader is everybody's hero. People say, "Isn't it wonderful what our leader accomplished? What a great person!" But when things aren't going so well, the leader becomes the scapegoat or the lightning rod. Those occasions can bring great distress to a leader. It's important to handle the stresses of leadership well and to recognize distress signals that might derail us and threaten our future.

In my third year as pastor, everything seemed to go wrong. Every change I made brought hailstorms of criticism, and virtually nobody talked about the good things that were happening. I was bombarded with bad news and bad attitudes. In my imagination, I pictured myself on a battlefield wearing just my underwear, burned up with holes in me, and smoke wafting off my weary body. My staff (of two people) and I sequestered ourselves in a Sunday school room and began to pray and worship God. The Lord was gracious to give us a special word. "You're *not* being defeated by the enemy. These things coming at you are nothing but pop guns and squirt guns. You are like an armored tank moving forward in My purposes."

If God rested after six days of creation, you need a rest too.

That was incredibly encouraging to me, and it changed my whole view of the stress I was experiencing.

Rest assured, you can't get rid of complainers or trouble. There's always somebody mumbling and sputtering when you're in leadership. You may be a Sunday school teacher, the leader of a youth choir, the care ministry coordinator, or the head janitor. Whoever you are in leadership, people will mumble and sputter at you. Don't believe any hype. When you become a Christian leader, all your problems *do not* end! (Oh, that they would!) Someone said the clearest evidence that you've really been anointed by the Holy Spirit for a leadership role is trouble! 2 Corinthians 1:8 says:

> For we would not, brethren, have you ignorant of our trouble which came to us in Asia, that we were pressed out of measure, above strength, insomuch that we despaired even of life.

You've faced pressures before, but God has a plan for relieving the stresses of leadership, and I'm going to share it with you in this chapter.

DEADLY FATIGUE

Moses was so distressed on some occasions that he wanted to quit altogether.

> Moses heard all the families standing around their tent doors weeping, and the anger of the Lord grew hot; Moses too was highly displeased. Moses said to the Lord, "Why pick on me, to give me the burden of a people like this? Are they *my* children? Am I their father? Is that why you have given me the job of nursing them along like babies until we get to the land you promised their ancestors?
>
> Where am I supposed to get meat for all these people? For they weep to me saying, 'Give us meat!' I can't carry this nation by myself! The load is far too heavy! If you are going to treat me like this, please kill me right now; it will be a kindness! Let me out of this impossible situation!"
>
> —Numbers 11:10-15 (TLB)

Here is one of the greatest leaders of all time feeling trapped in an impossible situation! The pressure mounted, and he felt hopeless and helpless, like there was no light at the end of the tunnel. Death, he said, would be the best way out.

When inner stresses are not properly drained out, they harm you physically. It's like taking a piece of tin and bending it back and forth, over and over. You may be able to bend it once or twice, but if you keep doing it relentlessly, it snaps.

A few years ago a flight for Aloha Airlines went terribly wrong. In midair, the airplane began creaking, and suddenly a big chunk of the cabin blew off. It was instant panic. One helpless flight attendant was mercilessly sucked out of the plane. Several passengers were hurt by flying debris, but the pilots miraculously landed the plane safely.

The reason for the problem? Metal fatigue. Airplanes have cycles; one cycle equals one takeoff and one landing. Every time an airplane flies, it undergoes stress from pressurizing and depressurizing, expanding and contracting. After so many cycles the metal gets overstressed and must be repaired or replaced. That's what happens to a human body when stress is not dealt with.

> *You've faced pressures before, but God has a plan for relieving the stresses of leadership.*

You're going to face pressures. All leaders face inner stresses that are caused by the outer pressures of life. The point is to not let them kill you.

A friend of mine was telling me about a 35-year-old man who was in charge of snow removal at a department store. Every night someone would keep their car parked in the parking lot so he couldn't shovel the snow in that spot. He had to leave a pile right around that car, and then the boss would scream at him for not having the parking lot completely shoveled out. One day, the young man didn't come home from work. They found him in his office, his head on his desk, dead of a massive heart attack. The likely cause was determined to be stress.

Doctors say stress is the number one killer of men between the ages of 35 and 39. Heart disease is related to stress. Stress is the leading culprit in headaches, tension, skin disease, high blood pressure, allergies, and psychosomatic illnesses. I'm quite certain stress plays a role in many more deaths than it's given credit for.

GOOD STRESS

But did you know some stress can be good? Think of a violin. Each string is tightened to a certain level of tension or stress, and when the stress is just right, it makes beautiful music. Overtighten, and it goes out of tune. Under-tighten, and it goes out of tune. There is a balance in which the right amount of stress tells us we're living life at its proper speed. On one hand we're not being lazy, and on the other hand we're not being overworked.

Picture a ladder. Each rung represents a different level in our Christian walk — different levels of leadership and challenge. If you're standing on one rung, the next rung up represents your next challenge. It causes some healthy stress as you exert yourself to climb to that next level. But if you're thinking ahead two rungs, the stress is too much. And if you stay on your current rung or step down a rung, you're not living up to your potential and you're in a comfort zone of boredom which leads to fatigue and lack of enthusiasm.

When inner stresses are not properly drained, they harm you physically.

Remember, the steps of a good man are ordered by the Lord — the steps, not the leaps (Psalm 37:23). Perhaps you're feeling unmotivated, bored. How about taking the next step in leadership! Create some healthy stress to replace the negative stress.

Symptoms Of Overstress

Here are some symptoms of overstress.

■ **Forgetfulness.** You go to the mall and can't remember where you parked. You have to beep the locks until you track down your car.

You leave your wallet home and insist that somebody stole it.

You get in your car to go somewhere...and forget where and why.

■ **Trouble seeing alternative actions.** You set your mind on one solution, and if a roadblock comes, you blow up or collapse. You can't see creative detours around problems.

■ **Trouble keeping pace.** You feel as though your life is like a sinking boat, and water is coming in faster than you can bail it out. You feel like you're in slow motion, unable to make headway against life's challenges.

■ **Temper flare-ups.** You are easily irritated and overreact to small things.

■ **An inability to change harmful patterns.** Bad habits come back or persist, and you can't seem to break them.

- **BUSYNESS.** Life becomes a never-ending treadmill of joy-less activity.

- **SLOPPINESS AND UNDEPENDABILITY BEGIN TO SET IN.**

- **A TRAPPED FEELING.** Your life is like a prison, and you want to run away from it all.

- **LOSS OF ORIGINAL INNER EXCITEMENT.** You lose your vision for the future.

- **STRANGE SLEEPING PATTERNS.** Your body needs more sleep, or you find it difficult to sleep even though you're tired. You don't want to go to bed at night, and you don't want to get up in the morning.

- **PASSIVITY.** You don't care what happens. You stop engaging in life.

- **FREQUENT BOUTS OF DEPRESSION.** You feel like a failure. There seems to be no reward in living. God seems far away or nonexistent.

- **BECOMING CYNICAL AND NEGATIVE.** You give up hope and become the world's resident skeptic. You honestly think nothing will ever get better, so what's the use of trying? You ridicule people who have hope.

- **PHYSICAL SYMPTOMS.** You get more colds than usual, chest pains, headaches, earaches, unusual jabs of pain, flare-ups of old problems. Some doctors believe stress accumulates and people can withstand only so much stress per lifetime. If they don't drain the stress tank, it reaches its limit, and they literally die, like the man in charge of snow removal.

Something gives out, blows out, quits working, and it's curtains, lights out, so long. That's why elderly people often die within a few months of their mate. The stress puts them over the limit.

How do you turn the valve and drain the stress out of life? The new breed of emerging leaders know. They've learned the secret of privacy and rest without feeling guilty about it.

POWER POINTS:

1. *Assess your stress level on this scale, 1 representing "no stress" and 10 representing "extreme stress."*

   1   2   3   4   5   6   7   8   9   10

2. *What are your "stress indicators?" Which signs of stress do you watch for in your life?*

3. *How have you dealt with stress up until now? Do you need to change your approach? Explain.*

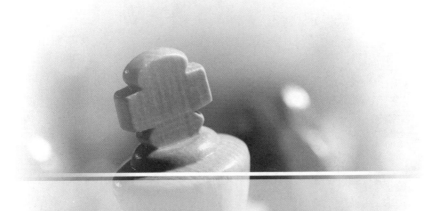

Grace touches man
deeper than a sermon or
lecture ever could.

CHAPTER 9

EMERGING LEADERS KNOW THE SECRET OF PRIVACY AND REST

A few years ago a friend and his wife came to our house for tea and talked to us about their little summer cabin in Arkansas. All they did there was grow vegetables and herbs and spend their days by the river worshiping the Lord in quiet. During another part of the year, they lived between California and Michigan, earning money with their painting business.

As I listened to them, something in my heart began to thirst. I thought, "If only I could retire and have a cabin in the woods like they do." I had very little privacy and rest at that time, and living in a "glass house" of leadership was starting to wear on me.

I'd gone to the store a few days earlier to buy food for my family's weekly movie night. My cart was loaded with chips, dip, and soda. As I was strolling down the aisle, a strange woman walked over to me and looking out of the corner of her eye, said, "Hello, Pastor." She looked in my cart, which was loaded with Pepsi, BBQ potato chips, sour cream potato chips, pretzels, chip dips and arrogantly sputtered, "So *that's* what you do with our tithe money." I wanted to run my basket into her knees! It was then I knew I needed a rest.

After my friends from Arkansas left, I figured out on paper that if I cashed in my pension and liquidated all my assets, including our house, I could retire for about seven years. After that I wouldn't know what to do. I figured Mary Jo and I could buy a cheap ranch in Arkansas and live for a while as semi-recluses without working. Something about the dream of privacy and rest sounded so intriguing and refreshing that I was almost willing to do anything to have it.

THE MANDATE OF REST

When I finally came back to reality, I realized I had learned something: Leaders need to rest. This is not optional. Mark 6:30 says:

> And the apostles gathered themselves together unto Jesus, and told him all things, both what they had done, and what they had taught.

They gave Jesus a report of how their ministry was going. Instead of saying (as I probably would say to my staff), "Good, now go double your efforts, we can do more." Jesus said:

> Come ye yourselves apart into a desert place, and rest a while: for there were many coming and going, and they had no leisure so much as to eat. And they departed into a desert place by ship privately.

—Mark 6:31-32

Amazing! In the time of great success, Jesus pointed out the mandate for rest. He lived a life of action, but He recognized the limits of the human frame and its need for regular rest and restoration. Some of you reading this book work six to seven days a week, at least twelve hours a day. You may not feel the effects of it now, but one day you'll break down and then understand why God created the principle of the Sabbath rest.

Overworked leaders tend to deal with stress in one of three unhealthy ways:

1. They go harder in the same direction and try to attack the problem head-on.

2. They direct their anger and frustration at a co-worker or loved one.

3. They turn on themselves and say, "I'm no good. If I was in God's will, I wouldn't be feeling like this."

But there's a healthy four-step prescription, and emerging leaders need to understand it.

■ 1. GET ALONE.

Paul said:

> Wherefore when we could no longer forbear, we thought it good to be left at Athens alone.

—I Thessalonians 3:1

Getting alone was Paul's deliberate strategy when the pressure was great. Privacy and rest.

Leaders need rest. This is not optional.

I did exactly the opposite in the first five years of my ministry, which is why I considered "cashing out" and quitting altogether. Everything I did was church, church, church. I had no diversion, no exercise routine, and I nearly killed myself as a result. Now I've learned the wisdom of getting alone as Paul did. Rather than taking that built-up pressure and unleashing it on someone else or denigrating myself, I get alone with God. I have a treadmill, and when the stress builds up, I walk on it. Or I go to the batting cages and put a quarter into the machine and take ten pitches, whacking them as hard as I can. Maybe your diversion will be to take a walk in the woods, lie out in the backyard and look at the stars, or drive to a hilltop somewhere. When you're alone, God can clean your vision and give you a fresh perspective.

■ 2. DELEGATE. Paul said in I Thessalonians 3:2, (and I paraphrase) "Timothy can take care of my business." As a leader, you may believe that nobody can do as good a job as you, and maybe you're right — but you're probably not. Part of your job is to develop people who can take the reins of your business or ministry so you can get away for a little while. You can't afford not to take a break. Stress builds up over time, and believe me, hospital rooms are more expensive than hotel rooms.

■ **3. DON'T BE SURPRISED WHEN PRESSURES COME.** Try to see God's purpose in your problems. He is using them to develop you.

> Dear brothers, is your life full of difficulties and temptations? Then be happy, for when the way is rough, your patience has a chance to grow.
>
> —James 1:2-3 (TLB)

> I will praise thee with my whole heart: before the gods will I sing praise unto thee. I will worship toward thy holy temple, and praise thy name for thy lovingkindness and for thy truth: for thou hast magnified thy word above all thy name. In the day when I cried thou answeredst me, *and* strengthenedst me *with* strength in my soul. All the kings of the earth shall praise thee, O LORD, when they hear the words of thy mouth. Yea, they shall sing in the ways of the LORD: for great is the glory of the LORD.

> Though the LORD *be* high, yet hath he respect unto the lowly: but the proud he knoweth afar off. Though I walk in the midst of trouble, thou wilt revive me: thou shalt stretch forth thine hand against the wrath of mine enemies, and thy right hand shall save me. The LORD will perfect *that which* concerneth me: thy mercy, O LORD, *endureth* for ever: forsake not the works of thine own hands.
>
> —Psalm 138:1-8

I get so tired of people seeing the devil in everything. Stress comes, and they automatically say, "That dirty devil is after me again." Thank God the devil *is* after you and not in front of you! I find that God is working somewhere in all my situations. That makes each challenge a joy and an opportunity.

■ 4. GET BACK TO WORK. After Paul got alone for a season, he went back to work. After a while, you can't pull the covers over your head anymore. It's time to re-enter the fray. If you're a teacher, get back to teaching. If you're a preacher, get back to preaching. If you're a prophet, get back to prophesying. If you're a Sunday school teacher, get back to Sunday schooling. If you're a fellowship group leader, get back to fellowshipping. Do what you're called to do!

Knowing that God is working in all our situations makes each challenge an opportunity.

WHY WE NEED REST

Some leaders aren't convinced they need to rest, even after hearing advice like this. So I want to offer a few reasons why privacy and rest are absolutely critical to a leader's long-term success. The new breed of emerging leaders knows this and practices it.

■ REST LETS US LISTEN TO GOD. Jesus got away from the crowds periodically. Leaders today want to constantly press forward and go for more success, so they neglect that time of rest and relaxation. But Jesus heeded the call to rest and retreat. He stayed in touch with His Father and had communion with Heaven.

Believe it or not our power and success comes *not* from our amazing exertions of our own power and energy but from God. If we lose touch with Him, all else is for naught. You need that infusion from Heaven; you need to see again the vision God has stamped on your heart. Otherwise your leadership and ministry are worth nothing.

- **REST AFFIRMS OUR HUMANITY.** God created everything in six days, and on the seventh day, He gave us an example: He rested. He didn't need to rest, but He was showing us how to live. Rest reminds us that our worth doesn't lie in our work but in our being loved by and made in the image of God.

- **REST KEEPS US HUMBLE.** We're not as indispensable as we imagine. Your company or church won't fall apart without you. Charles de Gaulle once said, "Graveyards are full of indispensable men." If you're a hardworking Sunday school teacher or youth worker, taking a week off out of every seven will preserve you in the long run. It humbles you.

> Pride *goeth* before destruction, and an haughty spirit before a fall.
>
> —Proverbs 16:18

Working too long without a break is a form of pride.

Often I lay on the floor in my office and look at the ceiling and talk with the Lord about anything that comes to mind. We have a casual, almost lazy conversation. We have fun together. I'm open with Him, and He's open with me. I call those times "creative loafing." In those restful, relaxing moments I learn more about what He wants me to do than when I'm constantly going one hundred miles per hour.

■ **REST HELPS OUR HEALTH.** A life without rest leads to exhaustion and physical breakdown. Blood tests show that exhausted people have higher amounts of a protein that causes blood to clot and dramatically minimizes blood flow to the heart and the brain. Lack of rest seems to contribute to cancer too. People in hot pursuit of career goals wear down their immune systems by overworking until eventually their bodies can't get rid of an out-of-control cell that becomes cancerous.

I expect my associate ministers to take vacations and days off. I want them to rest because I want them around for a long time! Even such great leaders as Evan Roberts in the Welsh revival and William Seymour of the Azusa Street revival burned out. Both became reclusive after their revivals shook the world. A life of action and activity demands privacy and rest.

Rest reminds us that our worth doesn't lie in our work but in our being loved by God.

Map out your rest schedule. Every seven weeks or so, take a mini-vacation. Every day, break away for a moment to be alone. Encourage your spouse and your family to have times and places of rest too. You'll love each other more for it!

Maybe you need to step outside right now and look at the stars or the scenery. It will help you consider your life in the grand scheme of God's creation. Successful generals know when not to go to battle as well as when to go. They know when the troops need "R & R." You can accomplish more in two hours of creative loafing before the Lord than you can in two years of exhausting work without knowing what the Lord wants.

Are you ready? Get resting!

The new breed of emerging leaders has no problem with this.

Next, we'll see another key attribute that emerging leaders of the twenty-first century possess.

POWER POINTS:

1. *Have you ever come close to burning out? What did you learn?*

2. *What changes do you need to make right now to your "time off" schedule? Do you have too few days off planned or too many? Be specific.*

3. *Where is your favorite place to go for rest and a vacation? Why?*

The new breed of
emerging leaders are perfectly
comfortable loving flawed,
mistake-ridden people.

CHAPTER 10

EMERGING LEADERS LOVE SINNERS

My daughter works for a newspaper, and keeps a file on some of the funny classified ads that appeared in newspapers around the country.

"Dinner Special – Turkey $2.35, Chicken or Beef $2.25, Children $2.00."

"For Sale: An antique desk suitable for lady with thick legs and large drawers."

"Stock up and save, limit one per customer."

"Man wanted to work in dynamite factory, must be willing to travel."

"Are you illiterate? Write today for free help."

A used car ad read, "Why go elsewhere to be cheated? Come here first."

Those are what you call "oops" moments.

Some major companies had "oops" moments when they advertised in other countries. Coca-Cola broke into the Chinese market as Ke-Ko-Kela, rendered in Chinese symbols, but after it was printed on all the bottles, they discovered the phrase meant "bite the wax tadpole!"

In Taiwan, Pepsi's slogan "Come alive with the Pepsi generation" translated as "Pepsi will bring your ancestors back from the dead."

Kentucky Fried Chicken's slogan "finger licking good" came out in Chinese as "eat your fingers off."

Parker Pen marketed a ballpoint pen in Mexico with ads that were supposed to say, "It won't leak in your pocket and embarrass you." But they mistakenly thought the Spanish word *embarazada* meant embarrass when it really means pregnant. As a result the ad read, "It won't leak in your pocket and make you pregnant."

> *If we're to be like God, we have to love sinners even before they're saved.*

And when General Motors introduced the Chevy Nova in South America, they didn't realize that "nova" in Spanish means "it won't go."[11]

---

[11] Morrison, Terri and Conaway, Wayne A., "Bite The Wax Tadpole", *Industry Week*, December 22, 1998

We all have "oops" in our lives. Big ones, small ones, and most sizes in between. Bill Cosby said, "You just don't want to hear the doctor say 'oops' when he's operating on you."

The problem for leaders is that we begin to think God doesn't allow "oops" moments. We press hard toward holiness and start demanding perfection of ourselves and others

> *The real answer is God's grace, not more human effort.*

forgetting that Jesus loves sinners — people who make mistakes, sometimes bad ones. Remember John 3:16, "For God so loved the world, that He gave His only begotten Son." If we're to be like God, we have to love sinners even before they're saved. The new breed of emerging leaders is perfectly comfortable loving flawed, mistake-ridden people.

COPS ON DUTY?

Jesus not only loves — He actually *likes* — sinners. Why does Jesus like sinners? Probably because self-righteous people are so miserable to be around! A professor at the University of Arizona was speeding down the highway, and a state patrolman pulled him over. The officer took pity on him and said, "I'll let you off the hook, but go slow, and drive safe." The professor corrected the cop's grammer, "That would be go slow, and drive safely. You said safe." The officer flipped open his notebook and issued him a $72 speeding ticket.

Self-righteous people are obnoxious!

I was sitting in a Chinese restaurant having a nice lunch with some other ministers. A lady walked over to our table and introduced herself. "Pastor Williams," she said, "I've seen you on television and heard you on the radio, and I want to thank you for your ministry." That was all. She walked away and sat down at her table. I finished my meal, and the waitress brought the fortune cookies over. I opened mine and started reading it. This lady stormed over and disgustedly said, "I can't believe a pastor would read a fortune cookie!" I jokingly shot back, "But this is where I get all my sermons." She huffed away, obviously annoyed.

Her attitude exemplifies the "cop on duty" attitude many Christian leaders carry with them. Instead of loving people as our first response, we judge them. We forget Ephesians 2:8-9, which says:

> For by grace are ye saved through faith; and that not of yourselves: *it is* the gift of God: Not of works, lest any man should boast.

When people make mistakes, we "old generation" leaders often exhort, "Try harder, and get it right next time." But the new breed of emerging leaders knows the *real* answer at that moment is God's grace, not more human effort.

GRACE ALERT

A single mother moved into a new neighborhood with her two children and enrolled them in a vacation Bible school. After the first day, the eight-year-old boy came home crying and feeling like an outcast. They had given ribbons for Bible memory verses, and he didn't know any, so he didn't get a ribbon. Some of the other kids had so many ribbons, they looked like peacocks strutting around. The teacher had told them, "Tomorrow we're going to give the grace ribbon that says, 'For by grace are ye saved through faith; and that not of yourselves: it is the gift of God.'" That night the two boys drilled each other to memorize it. The next day at VBS, they took their turn and recited the verse missing a few words here and there but getting the meaning right. The teacher said, "Boys, if you want this grace ribbon, you're going to have work harder." They went home empty-handed. She was blind to the contradiction in her own words.

That's how many leaders behave. We're willing to give grace...as long as people have done their part to earn it.

I was in a meeting of church leaders. During worship time, everyone was singing from their stationary spot in their pew except for a bearded man dancing madly down the aisles, waving his arms. I thought, "My goodness, how'd that kook get in here? Call the ushers!" Then I realized it wasn't a kook. It was the president of a major Christian university! He was dancing wildly, waving his arms in the air, and telling Jesus how much he loved Him. I was cut to the heart. I thought, "If he can do it, I can too." Right in front of all those ministers, I lifted my hands and danced around, and before I knew it, the ministers on the platform were lifting their hands and dancing too. It became a night of great gratitude to God for His grace and forgiveness.

> *Grace isn't just a one shot deal. I need it every day and so do you!*

But notice my first reaction: I wanted to boot the sinner from the meeting! It's as if I'd forgotten that I was a sinner too.

Sinners are often closer to receiving God's grace than so-called "saints."

The great theologian Karl Barth made a powerful statement: "We live solely by forgiveness." He meant, who can possibly satisfy the demands of the Holy God, a God that is so holy that no human can survive His presence? But through Jesus the price has been paid, and we're free to love God and enjoy His presence. It is a gift of God — and what a glorious gift!

When we love sinners we are actually loving ourselves. Mark Twain said, "Every human soul is like the moon. It has a dark side that people never see." I don't know if that's accurate, but even if it is, God sees that dark side, and His grace is sufficient for it.

A few years back I was on vacation in the Bahamas with my family. We went to the Atlantis hotel on Paradise Island. It's simply beautiful. They have glass tunnels you can walk through while sharks and all kinds of sea life swim around you. But to get to certain parts of the hotel, you have to walk through the casino. One morning we were making our way through the casino on our way to the aquarium. It was early and not a soul was there. Even though I have preached against gambling, I've always wanted to try a slot machine. My family was walking ahead of me, almost out of sight, and I thought, "If I reach in my pocket and there's a quarter, it'll be a sign." Sure enough there was a quarter. I looked around, squatted behind a slot machine, put a quarter in, and pulled that arm, thinking I'd never get caught. All of a sudden, lights flashed, "Ding, ding, ding, ding, ding, ding, ding, ding!" Sixty quarters dropped out of the machine. My family came back to get me, and I felt humiliated. I was so grateful for God's grace! I looked red-faced and sheepish. It was a clear reminder that grace isn't just a one shot deal. I need it every day and so do you! The hymn is correct: "It was grace that brought me safe this far, and grace will lead me home." If you're like me, you need grace now as much as ever.

SINNERS ARE REFRESHING!

Why did Jesus like sinners?

■ 1. BECAUSE THEY'RE NOT CHURCH-TRAINED, PRIM, AND PROPER. They don't feel the need to be right all the time.

■ 2. BECAUSE THEY KNOW THEY HAVE A PROBLEM. Self-righteous Christians congratulate themselves on the good job they've done. But sinners who know they're sinners don't set themselves so high in their own eyes.

■ 3. BECAUSE THEY KNOW THEY NEED A SAVIOR. When you're honest about your problem, you're close to the answer. Sinners are often closer to receiving God's grace than so-called "saints."

Hubert Humphrey, Lyndon Johnson's vice president, was bitter enemies with Richard Nixon, who beat Humphrey for the presidential race in 1968. But as Humphrey lay dying, after

Nixon had been disgraced by Watergate, he called Nixon and said, "I would like you to sit in the place of honor at my funeral, next to my wife." Humphrey had received Jesus Christ a month before. When asked why he'd invited Nixon to sit in the place of honor, Humphrey said, "From this vantage point, with the sun setting on my life, all the speeches, political conventions, and crowds, and fights are behind me now. I've concluded that when it's all said and done, what's really important in life is to experience God's grace, to forgive each other, and move on with life."

> *Emerging leaders don't give people lessons when they need grace.*

Grace touches men deeper than a sermon or a lecture ever could. Not once did a sinner come to Jesus Christ for grace and leave with a lecture. Genuine emerging leaders of this twenty-first century don't give people lessons when they need grace. They don't turn their noses up at sinners. Jesus likes sinners. He likes you too! Yes, it's easier to applaud judgment. We like to see God drowning Egyptians in the Red Sea and raining fire on Sodom and brimstone on Gomorrah. But God loves mercy more than judgement! He restored a psalmist-king who veered into adultery and murder. He took the Church's chief persecutor and turned him into a church-planter and author of half the New Testament. He has done the same thing in each of our lives, if we'll pause to remember it.

Maybe you need a fresh touch of God's grace. Maybe you're having trouble loving sinners. Return to the mercy that brought you to Jesus in the first place. Then you can worship God wildly, if you please. You can love God, love sinners, and shine forth the heart of Jesus. The new breed of emerging leaders loves sinners.

POWER POINTS:

1.   *What's your first feeling when confronted with an out-and-out sinner? Circle the words that describe it.*

   Disgust

   Anger

   Sadness

   Curiosity

   Mercy

   Love

   Compassion

2.   *When do you have a chance to be with non-Christians for an extended period of time? What are those situations like? Explain.*

3.   *How can you change your life so you're with sinners more often, and how can you treat them with greater grace than you do now? Write three things you intend to do differently.*

*F*aith knows the will of God,
prays the will of God,
and thanks God for the
fulfillment of it.

11
CHAPTER

EMERGING LEADERS UNDERSTAND AND OPERATE IN FAITH

Why is it that some leaders soar in life, their prayers get answered, and their dreams come true, while others pray and nothing ever happens? Their ministry stays small and sometimes seemingly insignificant to the very end.

Why can one Christian businessman believe the promises of God for success, and his business flourishes, and another Christian businessman bumps along barely making the payroll? It's not a prayer failure or a Bible-reading failure or a salvation failure but a *faith* failure. Those who have faith in God's Word soar. The possibilities are limitless. Those who stagger at the promises of God stagnate.

The new breed of emerging leaders takes God at His Word, acts in faith tenaciously, and sees God's promises become provisions in their lives and ministry. Their vision becomes reality; their dreams become true.

> What is faith? It is the confident assurance that something we want is going to happen. It is the certainty that what we hope for is waiting for us, even though we cannot see it up ahead.
>
> —Hebrews 11:1 (TLB)

> But without faith *it is* impossible to please *him*: for he that cometh to God must believe *that* he is, and that he is a rewarder of them that diligently seek him.
>
> —Hebrews 11:6

The one thing all successful leaders have in common is faith — genuine faith! Emerging leaders of the twenty-first-century Church have an extraordinary ability to operate in faith. They'll pull what they need out of the invisible realm into the visible realm — by faith. By faith they cause uncreated things — situations, circumstances, finances, or relationships — to be created. Their faith activates the power of God which will lead to exploits the world has not yet seen. Effective leaders are those who use their faith to turn God's promises into provisions.

> And we are anxious that you keep right on loving others as long as life lasts, so that you will get your full reward.
>
> Then, knowing what lies ahead for you, you won't become bored with being a Christian nor become spiritually dull and indifferent, but you will be anxious to follow the example of those who receive all that God has promised them because of their strong faith and patience.
>
> —Hebrews 6:11-12 (TLB)

Paul wrote about Abraham, the father of all who live by

faith. This passage contains dozens of golden nuggets for those in leadership.

> (As it is written, I have made thee a father of many nations,) before him whom he believed, *even* God, who quickeneth the dead, and calleth those things which be not as though they were.

> Who against hope believed in hope, that he might become the father of many nations, according to that which was spoken, So shall thy seed be.

> And being not weak in faith, he considered not his own body now dead, when he was about an hundred years old, neither yet the deadness of Sara's womb:

> He staggered not at the promise of God through unbelief; but was strong in faith, giving glory to God;

> And being fully persuaded that, what he had promised, he was able also to perform.

> And therefore it was imputed to him for righteousness.

> Now it was not written for his sake alone, that it was imputed to him;

> But for us also, to whom it shall be imputed, if we believe on him that raised up Jesus our Lord from the dead;

> Who was delivered for our offences, and was raised again for our justification.

> —Romans 4:17-25

Symptoms Of Weak Faith

When you lack faith, the symptoms show up in your spiritual and emotional life. These are the most common symptoms:

■ **SYMPTOM 1: CONSIDERING THE IMPOSSIBILITY OF A SITUATION.** Think of an "impossible situation" you've faced recently. Weak faith says, "This is a tough one. I doubt I can do anything about it." But the Bible says, "With faith nothing shall be impossible."

> And Jesus said unto them, Because of your unbelief: for verily I say unto you, If ye have faith as a grain of mustard seed, ye shall say unto this mountain, Remove hence to yonder place; and it shall remove; and nothing shall be impossible unto you.
>
> —Matthew 17:20

Which one did you say?

■ **SYMPTOM 2: LEANING ON FEELINGS.** People sometimes tell me, "I don't feel like I'm forgiven." I ask, "Did you confess your sins?" "Yes," they say, "but mine were too bad. I just don't feel forgiven." Three years later they're going around long-faced because they don't have the feeling they want. That's called carnality — going by your feelings instead of by what God's Word says.

Weak faith always says, "How do I feel today?" But the Bible says, "We walk not by sight (or senses), but by faith" (II Corinthians 5:7). "We look not at those things which are seen, but at those things which are unseen."

> While we look not at the things which are seen, but at the things which are not seen: for the things which are seen *are* temporal; but the things which are not seen *are* eternal.
>
> —2 Corinthians 4:18

One day I was scheduled to teach a class to ministry students in another city, but I didn't sleep well the night before. I never sleep well on trips because I'm a cuddler, and I like having Mary Jo with me. I woke up before 5 a.m. wishing I could skip the class or push back the time. But they were expecting me at 9:15 a.m., so I had no choice. As I got ready I remembered the verse that says:

> But if the Spirit of him that raised up Jesus from the dead dwell in you, he that raised up Christ from the dead shall also quicken your mortal bodies by his Spirit that dwelleth in you.
>
> —Romans 8:11

I stopped and prayed, "This mortal body hasn't had much sleep. God, You've got to pull me through this. I need the quickening power of the Holy Spirit." I walked into class a few hours later sharp and ready to go, and I announced, "This is going to be one of the best days of your life." The joy of the Lord bubbled out of me. After the session, students hugged me and thanked me, and the professor said they didn't usually do that. It was a great day. Faith had made it great!

■ SYMPTOM 3: NOT KNOWING THE WILL OF GOD. God's will is revealed largely through the Bible, and if you or I would possess every promise found in the Bible, the world would change rapidly. But His will is also revealed to us in specific, personal ways by the Holy Spirit, and at those times we must stand on the specific, personal revelation. The key is knowing God's will so you can exercise faith in it.

When our church in Lansing began to grow, the question arose about whether or not we should move to a different location. I didn't want to move. I liked where we were. But one night I had a dream. I was with my family driving a snowmobile, heading down the road toward a frozen lake. We came to a road, and the Holy Spirit said, "Turn right on that road." But first I decided to go straight ahead to the lake to spin circles on the ice, just for the thrill of it. I gunned the snowmobile and took all of us onto the lake, but almost immediately the ice cracked, and the snowmobile sank. I pulled myself out of the water, but I couldn't find my wife or my daughter. I saw my son's little hand sticking up out of the water, and I tried to pull him out. I was desperate and couldn't seem to rescue my family. My heart was pounding, and I sensed it was one of those dreams in which God was trying to speak to me.

> *Effective leaders are those who use their faith to turn God's promises into provisions.*

We had been considering a 43-acre piece of property on Creyts Road, but it was a complicated legal mess that I would rather have avoided. I needed an answer about God's will for the situation. The dream was one part, but I had to be sure. So one Saturday morning Mary Jo and I decided to pray for the answer together. We said, "God, we don't want to overextend the church. What do we do?" All of a sudden it was like a cloud lifted, and the Holy Spirit spoke to our hearts: "I want you to purchase the property." We had our answer. It wasn't what I wanted, but I was at peace with it. We bought the property and built the new church. Later I looked down the road where our old church had been, and I remembered the dream. The configuration of the roads was the same as in my dream, and if you turned right on Creyts Road where the Holy Spirit told me to turn, there was our new property. If we had stayed in that old building like I'd wanted, it would have been disastrous for our church and for my family.

The Holy Spirit speaks in many ways. When you have an opportunity, you will want to read my book, *"Have You Heard From The Lord Lately?"* [12]

Faith knows the will of God, prays the will of God, and thanks God for the fulfillment of it! Praying with no sense of God's will is a sign of weak faith. We should build our faith on His revelation to us through the Bible and through the word the Holy Spirit speaks personally

If you or I would possess every promise found in the Bible, the world would change rapidly.

to us. That revelation will guide us on the right path when questions or troubles arise.

Emerging twenty-first-century leaders walk in strong faith. Let's look at the signs of strong faith as exhibited in the life of Abraham, the father of all who would have faith.

---

[12] Williams, Dave, Dr., *Have You Heard From the Lord Lately?*, Decapolis Publishing, 2001, Lansing, MI

Signs Of Strong Faith

■ **Sign 1: Faith doesn't stagger.**

> He staggered not at the promise of God through unbelief...
>
> —Romans 4:20a

Staggering means to withdraw from, to be in disagreement with. Leaders stagger when they depart, in their hearts and minds, from the promises of God. Psalm 103:2 says:

> Bless the LORD, O my soul, and forget not all his benefits.

Wonderful benefits are attached to God's promises. God has made declarations and given wonderful promises; our job is to hold firm when it looks as though the promises aren't coming.

Early in the ministry, I made $125 a week — before tithes, offerings, and taxes. I took home $80, sometimes less, weekly. It took almost three weeks of pay just to make our house payment. One time our pantry got so empty that all we had were saltine crackers and a splash of milk. I had a baby daughter and no money. Did I stagger at the promises of God by withholding my tithes and offerings? I could have. Some people try to "loophole" God by creating exceptions. "We ran out of food. We knew you'd want us to buy food before we tithed, Lord."

The key is knowing God's will so you can exercise faith in it.

Well, our attitude was different. I was poor, but I didn't want to be a thief by withholding tithes and offerings. Still I felt depressed because I was unable to buy food for my family. I was ready to gripe when Mary Jo said, "We should praise and thank the Lord instead." We stood there in our tiny kitchen thanking God that His Word was more real than our situa-

Twenty-first-century leaders walk in strong faith.

tion. We got so excited! We found a durable inner reality that became greater than the "reality" we could see with our eyes.

Suddenly there was a knock at the door. A woman stood there with two big bags of groceries. "Brother Williams," she said, "I know you don't need these, and I'm embarrassed to even be here, but while I was shopping, the Holy Spirit told me to buy you two bags of groceries." We gratefully accepted them!

That's a true story, and it shows that God's promises are reliable. Our job is to stagger not!

- ### SIGN 2: FAITH GIVES GLORY TO GOD.

    ...but was strong in faith, giving glory to God.

    —Romans 4:20b

Abraham didn't sit around whining that the promise hadn't come to pass. He didn't complain saying, "God, I'm one hundred years old and pretty worn out. My wife went through menopause forty years ago. I don't know how you're going to give us a son." Rather he refused to talk about the impossibility and instead gave glory to God.

I've seen some parents beg God to save their children. I've seen others who show no outward sign of concern because they are confident in the promises of God. One prays in fear; the other prays in faith. The one who prays for hours in fear wonders why her prayers aren't answered, and the one who prays a few minutes in faith gets prayers answered! Giving glory to God is a sign that our faith is alive and active.

■ SIGN 3: FAITH IS FULLY PERSUADED.

> **And being fully persuaded that, what he had promised, he was able also to perform.**
>
> —Romans 4:21

Emerging leaders are fully persuaded of the promises of God, not relying on man's wisdom one iota. Their hearts are sold out, dead to any other logic, fully relying on what God — and God alone — has promised.

God's promises are reliable. Our job is to stagger not!

If you are fully persuaded, you will lead others to be fully persuaded too. The people in our congregation who attend on Sunday morning, Sunday night, and a midweek service never need counseling. Those who are not fully persuaded, who drop into church only once in a while, go in and out of counseling like it's a revolving door.

Faith comes by hearing the Word (Romans 10:17), not by hearing the *weird*. Some people add their own superstitions to what God has said. One woman told us she wouldn't come to church because the devil told her that if she did, he'd kill her son. Nonsense! But she was more persuaded of the devil's words than of God's almighty Word.

God is only impressed with our faith. When we stand on even the slightest bit of faith, God sees it and honors it.

Some Christians add their own words or works to the equation. I'm amazed to hear people pray for loved ones in trouble saying, "Oh Father, so-and-so got a bad report. You know how faithfully she served You over the past forty years and all she's done for so many people." As if God is impressed with her works! God is only impressed with our faith. Then His hand moves on our behalf. Forget all the good things you've done. Go on faith alone!

When we get beyond God's Word and into the weird, nothing works. When we get beyond God's Word and into our feelings, faith doesn't function. But when we stand on even the slightest bit of faith, God sees it and honors it. Our faith acts like a vacuum drawing His power. He loves rewarding our faith!

A lady who was paralyzed on one side of her body because of a stroke came to our church for prayer. We prayed for her, and she said, "Praise God! I'm healed." She didn't look healed, but she was fully persuaded by faith alone that she was. Her husband carried her to the car, and on the way home, her little finger that had been numb started tingling; then she regained feeling in her hand, then her arm, then her leg. By the time they got home, she popped out of the car jumping and leaping and praising God. God had honored her faith!

The one who prays in faith gets prayers answered!

It's your decision to be fully persuaded, your choice to have weak faith or strong faith. God has prepared a wonderful plan for you as a leader. He wants you to have whatever you want as it pertains to His Kingdom.

In the next chapter, we'll learn how to put that faith into action. I'll share the ABCs of accomplishing the impossible. The new breed of emerging leaders acts as if all things are possible. They operate in genuine faith.

POWER POINTS:

1. Assess your faith level. Do you operate in faith?

- *None of the time?*

- *Some of the time?*

- *Most of the time?*

2. *Write about a recent situation in which you exercised faith and saw it rewarded.*

3. *How can you grow your faith? Make a list of specific things you will do in the coming months to strengthen your faith.*

Once you have your aspiration and you believe it can come true, call on God to find out when it will come to pass.

CHAPTER 12

EMERGING LEADERS ACCOMPLISH THE "IMPOSSIBLE"

As a twenty-first-century leader, you will often face situations that seem impossible. It goes with the territory. But confronting and overcoming "impossibilities" is what ministry ought to be about!

Jesus taught much about turning impossibilities into possibilities. One time a man with a demon-possessed son brought the boy to Jesus' disciples. The man didn't recognize his son as being demon-possessed. He just thought he was a lunatic. The disciples couldn't do anything for him, so he brought the boy to Jesus who drove the demon out. Later Jesus commented on what He'd done. He told His disciples:

> Because of your unbelief: for verily I say unto you, If ye
> have faith as a grain of mustard seed, ye shall say unto
> this mountain, Remove hence to yonder place; and it
> shall remove...

—Matthew 17:20a

Jesus likened this boy's condition to a mountain.
Mountains symbolize obstacles, resistance, problems, and
challenges that keep us from a dream, desire, or promise. Jesus
went on to say:

> ...and nothing shall be impossible unto you.

—Matthew 17:20b

In speaking those words, He was speaking to all His fol-
lowers throughout history! Nothing, literally nothing, shall be
impossible for you and for me. But notice the qualifier —
faith. In the fulfillment of anything worthwhile, let alone the
fulfillment of an impossible dream, you will face mountains.
Some leaders see the mountain and run. Some see the mountain and camp out at the bottom and complain about the
mountain. But emerging leaders of the twenty-first-century
Church know how to move the mountain — by faith.

ABCs Of Mountain Moving

Here's an easy, alphabetical way to remember how to move
mountains.

■ "A" is for aspiration

To accomplish the impossible, you must have something
that resides in your heart (an aspiration, a dream,) and comes
from Heaven. Hebrews 11:1 says, "Faith is the substance of

things..." Things are objects or objectives. "Faith is the substance of things hoped for..." Hope is the aspiration, the picture, the dream. When our church was getting ready to build the Gilead Healing Center, our only evidence was faith. We didn't see the complex physically coming out of the ground, but there came a day when it did! We had pictures on the walls and brochures of what it would look like — that was our aspiration, our vision.

Emerging leaders know how to move the mountain – by faith.

God has put something on the heart of every sincere leader. For the sake of the people you lead, fulfill that dream! It has been said, "Be embarrassed to die until you've done something great for the sake of humanity!" Be a leader who leaves a legacy!

The problem is, most leaders have trouble determining which of their aspirations are from God and which are from their own imagination. We don't want to produce things that are going to become a thorn in our side years later. Jesus said:

> That which is born of the flesh is flesh; and that which is born of the Spirit is spirit.
>
> —John 3:6

And:

> ...every tree which bringeth not forth good fruit is hewn down, and cast into the fire.
>
> —Matthew 3:10b

We can sit around daydreaming and drawing out our dreams and journaling and planning, but if it's not God's dream, it's going to be fruitless. How do you know if it's God's dream? I've asked myself that question many times, and I discovered three "A"s for knowing whether an aspiration is from God.

- **NUMBER 1:** *ATTRACTION.* You'll be attracted to a certain thing. As a young Christian, I was attracted to preachers. I'd watch them and outline their messages. I'd try to figure out how they did it.

  What are you attracted to? If you're attracted to helping people, maybe you're called to be in medicine or social service. Or maybe music is your gift, or finances, or real estate. Find out what you're attracted to. God always gives us an attraction to something. That will help you define your aspiration.

- **NUMBER 2:** *APPETITE.* You'll have an appetite to learn more about whatever you're attracted to. It won't seem like work but pleasure much of the time.

- **NUMBER 3:** *ASTONISHING.* When God puts something on your heart, it's astonishingly big and appears impossible. Don't downsize your aspirations.

■ "B" IS FOR BELIEVING

Once you know your aspiration, believe you can accomplish it with God helping you, regardless of the odds against you. You may not see the outward manifestation of the dream yet, but you believe it's possible with God working with you because:

> **I can do all things through Christ which strengtheneth
> me.**
>
> —Philippians 4:13

If you're weak, He's going to give you strength. If you're poor, He's going to give you finances or show you how to get them. God's going to work on your behalf to fulfill your dream if you simply believe it.

Look at the men in the Bible: Moses was a stutterer, not very articulate. Yet God raised him up as a leader of two million adults, and he led them out of the land of bondage.

Gideon, the least in his family, had a low self-image and no self-esteem. Nonetheless he heard an angel of the Lord say, "I'm calling you to be a mighty man of valor." At first he couldn't even believe the angel was talking to him. "Who, me?" he asked. And yet he became a great deliverer of Israel (see Judges 6:11-8:35).

Paul was a learned Jew, a Pharisee of Pharisees, of the tribe of Benjamin. He understood Judaism through and through, and what did God do? Called him to preach to the Gentiles.

If it's not God's dream, it's going to be fruitless.

Peter was a Jew, but he lived more like a Gentile, and what did God do? He called him to reach the Jews. How does that work? I don't know, but God knows.

Nehemiah, the king's cupbearer, rebuilt Jerusalem's wall because God gave him an aspiration, and he believed he could do it with God's help.

Abraham came from a dysfunctional family, and God raised him up as the father of all those who would have faith.

The list goes on. Add yourself to it! Your background, education, culture, or ethnic heritage doesn't matter. What matters is getting a dream from God and believing it will come to pass based on His promises.

I was getting ready for Sunday services one morning, and Kenneth Copeland came on television. I conducted a funeral with Kenneth a few years ago. What a terrific fellow and a good teacher! But it wasn't always that way. Early in his life he was a grossly overweight nightclub singer. God took an overweight nightclub singer and turned him into a thin, fit, power-packed preacher. Kenneth didn't have anything going for him. He had so many debts; he didn't know how he'd ever get out except by faith. And now he doesn't have any debts. What happened? God raised him up to the level of his aspirations. Believe it! God will do it for you too!

> *When God puts something on your heart, it's astonishingly big and appears impossible.*

I have always admired Rex Humbard. I used to watch him on television and imitate his sermons. In 1987, I had the privilege of meeting Rex, and in 1989 he came to my office, knelt down with me, laid his hands on me, and prayed his anointing into me. He prayed that I would always stay sweet toward those who rise up against me, that I'd be a soul winner, and that many would come to Christ because of my leadership.

When people make excuses, they're limiting the Holy One!

Do you know where Rex comes from? He was the son of an itinerant preacher who had to put cardboard in his shoes to cover the holes because he couldn't afford to buy new shoes. Rex saw his daddy going from city to city, spending so much time traveling, wearing himself out, and this gave Rex a dream. He said, "Let's take the Gospel of Jesus on television around the world." Today he's known as the father of Gospel television, the first preacher to ever use satellite technology.

When people make excuses and say, "My education is wrong, my background is wrong, this is wrong, that is wrong," they're limiting the Holy One of Israel! There is no such thing as impossible with Him.

Creflo Dollar was a poor African-American boy with a dream to build a great church. People said, "You can't do it. You're the wrong color. It'll never happen for you — maybe for someone else, but not for you." Creflo didn't believe them. He had an aspiration; he believed he could do it. Today, 17,000 church members call Creflo their pastor.

And who hasn't heard of T.D. Jakes? People told him he was the wrong color to succeed, but he believed God's promises more than the voices of that "mountain." He had a dream. Today thousands of women have attended his "Women, Thou Art Loosed" conferences. Even unbelievers know who he is. He's been called the next Billy Graham by the secular media.

> *God will give you a plan, an idea, a novel solution.*

Kathryn Kuhlman was a farm girl with a failed marriage, but she had a dream from God and went on to become the greatest woman evangelist of the second half of the last century. Jesus didn't say, "Nothing shall be impossible unto you if you're the right color, the right culture, have the right educational background, or you have the right socioeconomic standing in the community." The only qualifier is *faith*, nothing else! We have to believe we can do something great.

HERE ARE TWO "B"S FOR BELIEVING.

- NUMBER 1: BASK IN THE PROMISES OF GOD BECAUSE THAT'S WHERE FAITH COMES FROM — THE WORD.

  So then faith *cometh* by hearing, and hearing by the word of God.

  —Romans 10:17

- NUMBER 2: BARRICADE YOUR HEART AGAINST DOUBTS AND CONTRARY EVIDENCE. I was amazed at all the contrary evidence that came at us when we said we were going to build a great healing center in Lansing. Every day a new problem arose: Where do we get the equipment? The personnel? The millions of dollars it will take to set up and run the center? But we barricaded our minds against doubt, and so the contrary words had no influence on us. Soon we received a large, unexpected donation from Blue Care Network that had closed some of their clinics; they gave us new medical equipment worth millions of dollars. We had so much that we shipped some to a ministry overseas. Now the center is operating, and it's everything we dreamed — and more. A huge stack of healing testimonies sit on my desk at this very moment.

Which evidence are you listening to? The evidence that says:

> But my God shall supply all your need according to his riches in glory by Christ Jesus.
>
> —Philippians 4:19

Or are you listening to contrary evidence? The answer makes all the difference in the world in your effectiveness as a twenty-first-century leader.

■ "C" IS FOR CALLING ON GOD!

Hebrews 11:6 says, "He is a rewarder of them that diligently seek Him."

Jeremiah 33:3, one of my favorite verses, says:

> Call unto me, and I will answer thee, and shew thee great and mighty things, which thou knowest not.

That's what God said! Once you have your aspiration and you believe it can come true, call on God to find out how it will come to pass. The steps of a righteous person are ordered by the Lord (Psalm 37:23). God will unfold how to do it! He'll give you a plan, an idea, a novel solution. Think of it like a road map that unfolds one section at a time. Your job is to follow the part of the road you can see until He unfolds the next panel of the map. Call on Him, and He'll show you great and mighty things.

There was a show on CBN many years ago called *"Don't Ask Me, Ask God!"* My kids made a career out of saying that to me. I'd ask, "David, how come your room isn't clean?" He'd reply, "Don't ask me, ask God!"

You don't have to fret or worry about anything.

But in many cases, that's just what we need to do. Naaman, the leper, needed to be healed, and so he came to the man of God to ask how (II Kings 5).

David the warrior, before he was king, needed to know how to defeat his enemies, and so he called on God and received an answer (I Samuel 23:2). I call that question-and-answer-type prayer. You give God a question, and you wait for an answer.

Mike Adkins was a Gospel singer, but he was having trouble selling his records. They were stacked up in his basement, so he asked God, "How do I promote my records?" This question was on his mind one day when he looked out the window and saw his neighbor Norman trying to start his lawnmower. Norman didn't shave, he was dirty, and had gross teeth. God spoke to Mike's heart and said, "Here's how you promote your records: Go help Norman start his lawnmower."

Mike argued with God and said, "But Lord, he's going to want to talk to me, and he stinks!" But God has a habit of not changing His orders. Finally Mike went over and asked, "Do you need some help?" Norman nodded, "Yeah." Mike cleaned the spark plug and started the lawnmower for Norman.

God's ways are not our ways, but He will answer when you call on Him with questions!

Then the Lord said, "Invite him over to watch the *700 Club* at your house," and Mike argued, "Oh no, he'll want to sit in my favorite chair and you know how he smells, Lord!" But Mike invited him over and Norman plopped right down into Mike's favorite chair, and at the end of the program, Mike asked, "Norman, would you like to have Jesus in your life?" Norman stuttered, "I really would."

Mike found out that Norman's mother had died when he was just a baby, and then later his father, who worked in the mines, was killed when a mine collapsed. Norman was left all alone to raise himself in a run-down house. Norman received Jesus in Mike's living room, and he and Mike became wonderful friends. Mike wrote a book about it and a song that says, "Norman, Jesus really loves you." Soon after Mike obeyed the Lord, people started ordering his records. He couldn't keep a big enough supply. They became some of the best selling Gospel records in the 1970s and early 1980s. And it started when God told him to help the man across the street.

God's ways are not our ways, but He will answer when you call on Him with questions! He will show you great and mighty things (Jeremiah 33:3).

HERE ARE THREE "C"S FOR CALLING ON GOD AND GETTING RESULTS:

- NUMBER 1: COME TO GOD.

  > But without faith *it is* impossible to please *him*: for he *that* cometh to God must believe that he is, and that he is a rewarder of them that diligently seek him.
  >
  > —Hebrews 11:6

  > Come unto me, all *ye* that labour and are heavy laden, and I will give you rest.
  >
  > —Matthew 11:28

  > All that the Father giveth me shall come to me; and him that cometh to me I will in no wise cast out.
  >
  > —John 6:37

- NUMBER 2: BE CANDID WITH GOD (see John 4:24). Don't put on your prayer talk. Don't give a speech. Speak in a normal way and from your heart.

- NUMBER 3: CALMLY REST IN GOD'S ABILITY TO GIVE YOU EVERYTHING YOU NEED TO ACCOMPLISH THE IMPOSSIBLE (see Hebrews 4). You don't have to fret or worry about anything. Just hang out with God, and be calm.

Let us therefore fear, lest, a promise being left *us* of entering into his rest, any of you should seem to come short of it.

For unto us was the gospel preached, as well as unto them: but the word preached did not profit them, not being mixed with faith in them that heard *it*.

—Hebrews 4:1-2

But my God shall supply all your need according to his riches in glory by Christ Jesus.

—Philippians 4:19

Don't worry about anything; instead, pray about everything; tell God your needs, and don't forget to thank him for his answers.

—Philippians 4:6 (TLB)

There's one more letter in our ABCs study.

■ "D" IS FOR DO IT!

James 2:26 says faith without action is dead. You've got to *do* something to act on your aspiration. Don't sit around waiting for someone else to do it for you.

Dare to launch out!

Delay your lesser desires!

Decree your success based on God's Word and God's promises!

My friend, Cheryl Prewitt (now Cheryl Salem), did just that. As a little girl in Choctaw, Mississippi, she had an aspiration to become Miss America so she could be a leading voice for God. But a terrible car accident cut up her face and crushed her leg so that it never grew like the other one. She walked with a heavy limp. It looked like her dream was shattered, but she said, "God, in spite of this physical challenge, somehow I'm going to be Miss America."

She began reading and meditating on Mark 11:23:

> For verily I say unto you, That whosoever shall say unto this mountain, Be thou removed, and be thou cast into the sea; and shall not doubt in his heart, but shall believe that those things which he saith shall come to pass; he shall have whatsoever he saith.

She knew she'd have to overcome her funny southern accent, the scars on her face, and her short leg. One night she went to a church meeting and told all her friends, "Tonight my leg's going to grow." She walked in limping, received prayer, and walked out without a limp. She got her miracle. The scars on her face diminished. She went on to become Miss Mississippi after several tries and then went to the Miss America pageant. She was poor and couldn't afford a sequined dress like everybody else, so she bought a Kmart dress, and she and her sister stayed up all night, gluing sequins to it with Elmer's glue.[13]

There's no aspiration too high for those in Christ Jesus.

---

13 Salem, Cheryl, *Bright and Shining Place*, Harrison House, 1987, Tulsa, OK

Don't you ever tell me that there's something preventing you from reaching your dream! If you have the determination to do it, the tenacity to stick to it, learn to blast through the resistance and opposition, you'll make it happen!

Cheryl was crowned Miss America 1980 and walked that runway just as beautiful as could be, and for a whole year, she went around the country telling people what God had done for her.

There's no aspiration too high for those of us who are in Jesus Christ! Set your mind and heart on your aspiration, believe it will happen, call on God, and then *do it*, and you'll walk onto the pages of history.

POWER POINTS:

1. *What is your aspiration as a leader? What is your impossible dream? Write it down.*

2. *How have you believed God and called on Him to see this aspiration accomplished? Do you need to improve in these areas? Explain.*

3. *What are you doing to fulfill your aspiration? What more could you do?*

R*aise up a successor*
to continue the work God
began in you.

13

EMERGING LEADERS PLAN TO LEAVE A LEGACY

As we approach the end of this book, we come to one of the most enduring traits of a twenty-first-century leader: *He or she leaves a legacy.*

The saddest thing in the world would be for your work to evaporate the moment you go to Heaven. A leader by definition leaves behind an imprint of his or her efforts. Think of the great Christian organizations like the Salvation Army, the Billy Graham Association, and many church denominations which are continuing the work of their founders. At some level every authentic leader aspires to leave that kind of "ministry with momentum" when they go to be with the Lord.

Moses left one of the greatest legacies in history. He lived in an atmosphere of the miraculous like no one else has. He led the children of Israel out of bondage to Egypt. He talked with God face-to-face, and when he came down from the mountain, his own face shone so brightly that he had to wear a veil to keep from blinding people.

The saddest thing in the world would be for your work to evaporate the moment you go to Heaven.

At 120 years old, Moses' life drew to a close, but before he left, he appointed his successor Joshua (see Deuteronomy 34:9). Moses knew the people would not flourish on memories alone. They needed a flesh-and-blood human being to lead them. This is the first and most critical part of leaving a legacy: *Raise up a successor to continue the work God began in you.*

Every emerging leader is concerned about raising up a successor. Whatever you do, wherever you work — in ministry, business, education, the military, or any other sector of society — you must raise up a "Joshua" whom you can turn things over to one day.

Some mediocre leaders tell me they're too busy to train other people in the ministry. Hogwash! I have no sympathy for that complaint. If you're working 150 hours a week, you're working wrong. If you would simply invest a fraction of that time training leaders, your effectiveness would grow exponentially while your workload shrinks. The Word of God says that genuine leaders equip believers for the work of the ministry.

And he gave some, apostles; and some, prophets; and some, evangelists; and some, pastors and teachers;

> For the perfecting of the saints, for the work of the ministry, for the edifying of the body of Christ:

> —Ephesians 4:11-12

Raising up a successor must be on the list of primary goals for every emerging leader in this twenty-first century. Don't ever sacrifice this for short-term gain. Pray about it, aspire to accomplish it, have faith that it will happen. God will honor your efforts.

THE LAYING ON OF HANDS

God chose Joshua to succeed Moses, and Moses laid his hands on Joshua:

> And Joshua the son of Nun was full of the spirit of wisdom; for Moses had laid his hands upon him...

> —Deuteronomy 34:9a

Moses didn't lay hands on anyone else to pass on the mantle of leadership. This tells us something: be discriminating about who you lay hands on to impart authority.

There is something supernatural and sacred about the laying on of hands for the impartation of authority. The Bible says not to lay hands on people suddenly or prematurely (I Timothy 5:22). I will lay hands on people to send them out under the auspices of Mount Hope Church. I will lay hands on anybody to pray for them, but I will not lay hands on just anybody to impart my God-given authority into their life.

There is something supernatural and sacred about the laying on of hands for the impartation of authority.

One Wednesday night, two people came up to me after service and asked me to lay hands on them to transfer my authority and anointing to them. First, a precious lady came up, and she seemed very nice. I had no idea who she was. She introduced herself, and she said that God told her to come up and tell me to lay hands on her and to transfer my authority and anointing into her. I was very uncomfortable because I didn't know her. Can you imagine Moses deciding to lay his hands on just anybody he didn't know? I said, "I am sorry. I will lay my hands on you and pray a general prayer, but I won't impart anointing to you because I don't know you." She said, "Oh, that's fine."

Right after that another lady came up and said, "I'm from another state, and I'm coming up to have you lay hands on me because I want you to transfer your anointing into me because you are justice. And, Mary Jo, I want her to lay hands on me and transfer her anointing into me because she is mercy. I need a touch of justice and mercy. I want you to transfer the anointing of this whole church into my life, so I can take it back to where I'm going." Again uncomfortably, I had to say I wouldn't do that.

But God will raise up proper leaders under you whom you can train, encourage, and prepare to take over when you move on. They are the ones who will receive the mantle of your authority, like Elisha received Elijah's.

LEADERS AND THEIR SUCCESSORS

Smith Wigglesworth, a twentieth-century apostle of faith, was in his eighties when he went to Heaven. Before he did, young Lester Sumrall stood in his house in England, and Wigglesworth said, "Young man, let me tell you some of the things you are going to see in your lifetime." He told Lester things concerning the great revival of the sixties and seventies that would come. He prophesied of Christ's return and the catching away of the Church and some of the signs that would take place in England and Australia before the coming of Christ. With tears in his eyes, he asked young Lester

God will raise up proper leaders whom you can train, encourage, and prepare to take over when you move on.

to kneel in front of him, Smith put his hands on Lester's head and prayed to impart his anointing into him. Lester didn't feel anything, but he was a man of faith; he didn't have to feel anything. He left there and went to the Philippines. He cast out devils and healed the sick and preached the Gospel to tens of thousands in foreign nations before he came back to America to be a pastor. Sumrall laid hands on a couple of young men before he died. They both have powerful ministries today.

When Katheryn Kuhlman ministered, there was a beautiful atmosphere of miracles in her services, but she didn't lay hands on anyone to carry on her ministry. At the age of sixty-eight, with an enlarged heart, she lay in a hospital bed, and Oral Roberts called her and said, "I see darkness all around you. From eternity a shaft of light is coming in to dispel the darkness." She just said, "I know, Oral, I know." That night her whole room lit up, a glow came to her face, and the Father leaned down and kissed her, and she went to Heaven.[14]

> *Who will carry on your work after you're gone?*

But she hadn't imparted her authority to anybody, and so for many years, there was no great miracle ministry. There were people who tried, but everyone seemed to fail. But a young, long-haired evangelist from Canada, originally an immigrant, had seen Kuhlman. He confessed that he had somewhat backslid after her death; he was cold in his heart. She had not transferred her anointing to him, but he began studying her to understand the heartbeat of her ministry. One day the Holy Spirit came on him and said, "I will anoint you to do the same thing." So he set up a miracle service in his

---

[14] Roberts, Oral, *Abundant Life Magazine*, April, 1976, Tulsa, OK

church to start with, and today he goes all over the world holding miracle services that have even eclipsed Kuhlman's miracle services. His name is Benny Hinn.[15]

Moses imparted his authority to Joshua. Smith transferred it to Lester. Lester transferred it to others. Who will carry on your work after you're gone?

I am believing that God will give every leader reading this book a long and fruitful life here on earth. But when you get to be 120 years old, if God reaches down and kisses you, make sure there is a successor ready to take the vision and run with it for another lifetime. That's how you can leave a legacy of leadership.

POWER POINTS:

1. *Are you cultivating a successor? Who? Why have you chosen this person?*

2. *If you could write what people say about you at your funeral, what would you write? What do you think they will say about your legacy?*

3. *How can you ensure that the legacy you leave is strong and long-lasting? Write three changes you intend to make to ensure you leave a lasting legacy.*

---

[15] Hinn, Benny, Taped message to leaders at Orlando Christian Center, 1982, Orlando, FL

*This is the greatest time
in history to be a
church leader.*

THE LAST WORD

If I could sit face-to-face with you and every other leader reading this book, I would encourage you with the knowledge that God has given you a call and a destiny! Don't doubt it. Don't let the devil tell you otherwise. God will equip you and establish you in your calling. I exhort you.

- Have faith

- Practice the discipline of fasting

- Get proper rest, and avoid the stress that comes so easily with your position of leadership

I STRONGLY ENCOURAGE YOU TO

- Know what you want and ask for it specifically

- Accept responsibility

- Avoid distractions

- Love sinners

- Leave a legacy

- Accomplish the impossible

If you do these things, you will indeed walk onto the pages of history. You will be known as a true twenty-first-century pacesetter.

This is the greatest time in history to be a church leader. Never has there been such an open door for the work of God on this planet. *This is your day!* It's time to seize your destiny as an emerging twenty-first-century leader whose life and legacy testifies of God's awesome power to accomplish the impossible!

You are God's chosen leader! This is your time! *Go for it!*

ABOUT
THE AUTHOR
AND RELATED
MINISTRIES

ABOUT THE AUTHOR

Dr. Dave Williams is pastor of Mount Hope Church and International Outreach Ministries, with world headquarters in Lansing, Michigan. He has served for over 20 years, leading the church in Lansing from 226 to over 4000 today. Dave sends trained ministers into unreached cities to establish disciple-making churches, and, as a result, today has "branch" churches in the United States, Philippines, and in Africa.

Dave is the founder and president of Mount Hope Bible Training Institute, a fully accredited institute for training ministers and lay people for the work of the ministry. He has authored over 55 books including the fifteen-time best seller, *The New Life...The Start of Something Wonderful* (with over 2,000,000 books sold), and more recently, *The Miracle Results of Fasting*, *The Road To Radical Riches,* and *Angels-They Are Watching You!*

The Pacesetter's Path telecast is Dave's weekly television program seen over a syndicated network of secular stations, and nationally over the *Sky Angel* satellite system. He is also seen worldwide on the *TCT* Satellite System, receiving over 1,000 salvation calls to the prayer center weekly. Dave has produced over 125 audio cassette programs including the nationally acclaimed *School of Pacesetting Leadership* which is being used as a training program in churches around the United States, and in Bible Schools in South Africa, South America, Mexico, and the Philippines. He is a popular speaker at conferences, seminars, and conventions. His speaking ministry has taken him across America, Africa, Europe, Asia, and other parts of the world.

Along with his wife, Mary Jo, Dave established The Dave and Mary Jo Williams Charitable Mission (Strategic Global Mission), a mission's ministry for providing scholarships to pioneer pastors and grants to inner-city children's ministries.

He travels with his family and enjoys vacationing in Florida. Dave and Mary Jo own *Sun Prime Equities*, a Florida island condo enterprise.

Dave received his doctorate of ministry from Pacific International University in 2004.

Dave's articles and reviews have appeared in national magazines such as *Advance*, *The Pentecostal Evangel*, *Ministries Today*, *The Lansing Magazine*, *The Detroit Free Press* and others.

During his time of study, he developed curriculum for *The School for Intercessors* and *The School of Successful Church Planting*. Both are being taught in churches across the United States. Dave, as a private pilot, flies for fun. He is married, has two grown children, and lives in Delta Township, Michigan.

You may write to Pastor Dave Williams:

P.O. Box 80825

Lansing, MI 48908-0825

Please include your special prayer requests when you write, or you may call the Mount Hope Global Prayer Center: (517) 327-PRAY

For a catalog of products, call:

1-517-321-2780 or

1-800-888-7284

or visit us on the web at:

www.mounthopechurch.org

Gilead Healing Center

Gilead
HEALING CENTER

- **The Place Of Another Chance**
- **Training For The Healing Ministry**

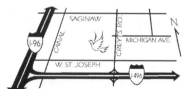

- *Prayer*
- *Nutrition*
- *Counseling*
- *Medical*

517-321-2780

We're here for you!
Lansing, Michigan

When you face a struggle...
When you need a miracle...

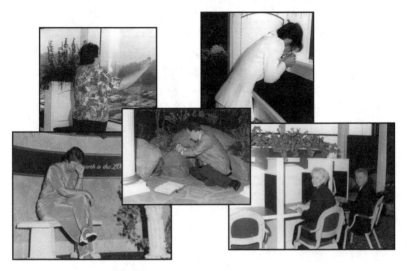

...we'll stand with you in prayer.

GLOBAL PRAYER CENTER

We believe Jesus Christ is the same yesterday, today, and forever (Hebrews 13:6).

Our prayer partners will agree with you in prayer for your miracle (Matthew 18:18-19).

Call Anytime
(517) 327-PRAY

The Mount Hope Global Prayer Center in Lansing, Michigan

OTHER OFFERINGS FROM DECAPOLIS PUBLISHING

FOR YOUR SPIRITUAL GROWTH

Here's the help you need for your spiritual journey. These books will encourage you, and give you guidance as you seek to draw close to Jesus and learn of Him. Prepare yourself for fantastic growth!

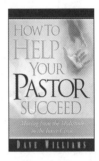

HOW TO HELP YOUR PASTOR SUCCEED
You are an important key to the success of your pastor and your church.

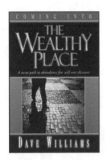

COMING INTO THE WEALTHY PLACE
You can live on the concierge level of life. Release the power in your life for genuine prosperity.

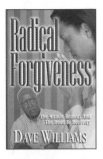

RADICAL FORGIVENESS
This "how to" book shows how to be released from offenses, hurts, and the tormenting pain of unforgiveness.

RADICAL HEALING
It's time to start living in God's promise of good health that Jesus bought for you on the Cross.

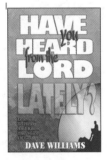

HAVE YOU HEARD FROM THE LORD LATELY?
You will discover that there are many ways God speaks today.

THE PRESENCE OF GOD
Find out how you can have a more dynamic relationship with the Holy Spirit.

These and other books available from Dave Williams and:

DECAPOLIS PUBLISHING

FOR YOUR SPIRITUAL GROWTH

Here's the help you need for your spiritual journey. These books will encourage you, and give you guidance as you seek to draw close to Jesus and learn of Him. Prepare yourself for fantastic growth!

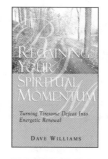

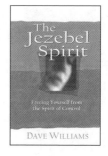

RADICAL FASTING
How would you like to achieve your dreams at "break-neck" speed? Radical fasting may be your key!

REGAINING YOUR SPIRITUAL MOMENTUM
Use this remarkable book as your personal street map to regain your spiritual momentum.

THE JEZEBEL SPIRIT
Do you feel controlled? Learn more about what the Bible says about this manipulating principality's influence.

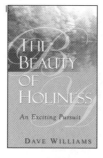

DEVELOPING THE SPIRIT OF A CONQUEROR
Take back what the enemy has stolen from you. Learn how to engage your authority and Develop the Spirit of a Conqueror.

BEAUTY OF HOLINESS
We face the choice — holiness or rebellion. True holiness comes about by working together in cooperation with the Holy Spirit.

ABCs OF SUCCESS & HAPPINESS
God wants to give you every good gift, so it's time to accept the responsibility for your success today!

These and other books available from Dave Williams and:

DECAPOLIS PUBLISHING

FOR YOUR SPIRITUAL GROWTH

Here's the help you need for your spiritual journey. These books will encourage you, and give you guidance as you seek to draw close to Jesus and learn of Him. Prepare yourself for fantastic growth!

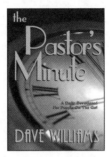

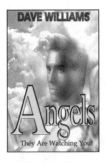

QUESTIONS I HAVE ANSWERED
Get answers to many of the questions you've always wanted to ask a pastor!

THE PASTOR'S MINUTE
A daily devotional for people on the go! Powerful topics will help you grow even when you're in a hurry.

ANGELS: THEY ARE WATCHING YOU!
The Bible tells more than you might think about these powerful beings.

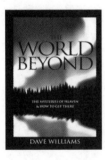

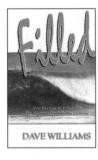

THE WORLD BEYOND
What will Heaven be like? What happens there? Will we see relatives who have gone before us? Who REAL-LY goes to Heaven?

FILLED!
Learn how you can be filled with the mightiest power in the universe. Find out what could be missing from your life.

STRATEGIC GLOBAL MISSION
Read touching stories about God's plan for accelerating the Gospel globally through reaching children and training pastors.

These and other books available from Dave Williams and:

DECAPOLIS PUBLISHING

FOR YOUR SPIRITUAL GROWTH

Here's the help you need for your spiritual journey. These books will encourage you, and give you guidance as you seek to draw close to Jesus and learn of Him. Prepare yourself for fantastic growth!

HOW TO BE A HIGH PERFORMANCE BELIEVER
Pour in the nine spiritual additives for real power in your Christian life.

SECRET OF POWER WITH GOD
Tap into the real power with God; the power of prayer. It will change your life!

THE NEW LIFE . . .
You can get off to a great start on your exciting life with Jesus! Prepare for something wonderful.

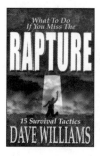

MIRACLE RESULTS OF FASTING
You can receive MIRACLE benefits, spiritually and physically, with this practical Christian discipline.

WHAT TO DO IF YOU MISS THE RAPTURE
If you miss the Rapture, there may still be hope, but you need to follow these clear survival tactics.

THE AIDS PLAGUE
Is there hope? Yes, but only Jesus can bring a total and lasting cure to AIDS.

These and other books available from Dave Williams and:

DECAPOLIS PUBLISHING

FOR YOUR SPIRITUAL GROWTH

Here's the help you need for your spiritual journey. These books will encourage you, and give you guidance as you seek to draw close to Jesus and learn of Him. Prepare yourself for fantastic growth!

THE ART OF PACESETTING LEADERSHIP
You can become a successful leader with this proven leadership development course.

GIFTS THAT SHAPE YOUR LIFE
Learn which ministry best fits you, and discover your God-given personality gifts, as well as the gifts of others.

GROWING UP IN OUR FATHER'S FAMILY
You can have a family relationship with your heavenly father. Learn how God cares for you.

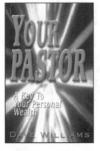

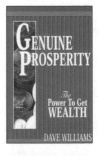

SUPERNATURAL SOULWINNING
How will we reach our family, friends, and neighbors in this short time before Christ's return?

YOUR PASTOR: A KEY TO YOUR PERSONAL WEALTH
By honoring your pastor you can actually be setting yourself up for a financial blessing from God!

GENUINE PROSPERITY
Learn what it means to be truly prosperous! God gives us the power to get wealth!

These and other books available from Dave Williams and:

DECAPOLIS PUBLISHING

FOR YOUR SPIRITUAL GROWTH

Here's the help you need for your spiritual journey. These books will encourage you, and give you guidance as you seek to draw close to Jesus and learn of Him. Prepare yourself for fantastic growth!

SOMEBODY OUT THERE NEEDS YOU
Along with the gift of salvation comes the great privilege of spreading the Gospel of Jesus Christ.

SEVEN SIGNPOSTS ON THE ROAD TO SPIRITUAL MATURITY
Examine your life to see where you are on the road to spiritual maturity.

THE PASTOR'S PAY
How much is your pastor worth? Who should set his pay? Discover the scriptural guidelines for paying your pastor.

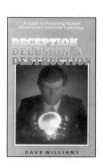

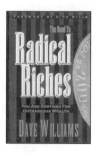

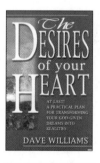

DECEPTION, DELUSION & DESTRUCTION
Recognize spiritual deception and unmask spiritual blindness.

THE ROAD TO RADICAL RICHES
Are you ready to jump from "barely getting by" to God's plan for putting you on the road to Radical Riches?

THE DESIRES OF YOUR HEART
Yes, Jesus wants to give you the desires of your heart, and make them realities.

These and other books available from Dave Williams and:

FOR YOUR SUCCESSFUL LIFE

These video cassettes will give you successful principles to apply to your whole life. Each a different topic, and each a fantastic teaching of how living by God's Word can give you total success!

THE PRESENCE OF GOD
Find out how you can have a more dynamic relationship with the Holy Spirit.

FILLED WITH THE HOLY SPIRIT
You can rejoice and share with others in this wonderful experience of God.

GIFTS THAT CHANGE YOUR WORLD
Learn which ministry best fits you, and discover your God-given personality gifts, as well as the gifts of others.

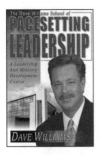

THE SCHOOL OF PACESET-TING LEADERSHIP
Leaders are made, not born. You can become a successful leader with this proven leadership development course.

MIRACLE RESULTS OF FASTING
Fasting is your secret weapon in spiritual warfare. Learn how you'll benefit spiritually and physically! Six video messages.

A SPECIAL LADY
If you feel used and abused, this video will show you how you really are in the eyes of Jesus. You are special!

These and other videos available from Dave Williams and:

FOR YOUR SUCCESSFUL LIFE

These video cassettes will give you successful principles to apply to your whole life. Each a different topic, and each a fantastic teaching of how living by God's Word can give you total success!

HOW TO BE A HIGH PERFORMANCE BELIEVER
Pour in the nine spiritual additives for real power in your Christian life.

THE UGLY WORMS OF JUDGMENT
Recognizing the decay of judgment in your life is your first step back into God's fullness.

WHAT TO DO WHEN YOU FEEL WEAK AND DEFEATED
Learn about God's plan to bring you out of defeat and into His principles of victory!

WHY SOME ARE NOT HEALED
Discover the obstacles that hold people back from receiving their miracle and how God can help them receive the very best!

BREAKING THE POWER OF POVERTY
The principality of mammon will try to keep you in poverty. Put God FIRST and watch Him bring you into a wealthy place.

HERBS FOR HEALTH
A look at the concerns and fears of modern medicine. Learn the correct ways to open the doors to your healing.

These and other videos available from Dave Williams and:

DECAPOLIS PUBLISHING

RUNNING YOUR RACE

These simple but powerful audio cassette singles will help give you the edge you need. Run your race to win!

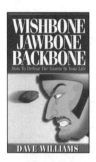

LONELY IN THE MIDST OF A CROWD
Loneliness is a devastating disease. Learn how to trust and count on others to help.

HERBS FOR HEALTH
A look at the concerns and fears of modern medicine. Learn the correct ways to open the doors to your healing.

HOW TO GET ANYTHING YOU WANT
You can learn the way to get anything you want from God!

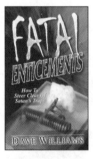

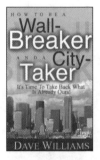

WISHBONE, JAWBONE, BACKBONE
Learn about King David, and how his three "bones" for success can help you in your life quest.

FATAL ENTICEMENTS
Learn how you can avoid the vice-like grip of sin and it's fatal enticements that hold people captive.

HOW TO BE A WALL BREAKER AND A CITY TAKER
You can be a powerful force for advancing the Kingdom of Jesus Christ!

These and other audio tapes available from Dave Williams and:

DECAPOLIS PUBLISHING

EXPANDING YOUR FAITH

These exciting audio teaching series will help you to grow
and mature in your walk with Christ. Get ready for amazing
new adventures in faith!

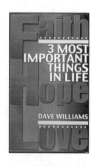

THE BLESSING
Explore the many ways
that God can use you to
bless others, and how He
can correct the missed
blessing.

SIN'S GRIP
Learn how you can avoid
the vice-like grip of sin
and its fatal enticements
that hold people captive.

FAITH, HOPE, & LOVE
Listen and let these three
"most important things in
life" change you.

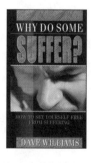

**PSALM 91
THE PROMISE OF
PROTECTION**
Everyone is looking for
protection in these per-
ilous times. God promises
protection for those who
rest in Him.

**DEVELOPING
THE SPIRIT OF A
CONQUEROR**
You can be a conqueror
through Christ! Also,
find out how to keep
those things that you
have conquered.

WHY DO SOME SUFFER
Find out why some people
seem to have suffering in
their lives, and how to
avoid it in your life.

*These and other audio tapes
available from Dave Williams and:*

DECAPOLIS
PUBLISHING

EXPANDING YOUR FAITH

These exciting audio teaching series will help you to grow and mature in your walk with Christ. Get ready for amazing new adventures in faith!

ABCs OF SUCCESS AND HAPPINESS
Learn how to go after God's promises for your life. Happiness and success can be yours today!

FORGIVENESS
The miracle remedy for many of life's problems is found in this basic key for living.

UNTANGLING YOUR TROUBLES
You can be a "trouble untangler" with the help of Jesus!

HOW TO BE A HIGH PERFORMANCE BELIEVER
Put in the nine spiritual additives to help run your race and get the prize!

BEING A DISCIPLE AND MAKING DISCIPLES
You can learn to be a "disciple maker" to almost anyone.

HOW TO HELP YOUR PASTOR & CHURCH SUCCEED
You can be an integral part of your church's & pastor's success.

These and other audio tapes available from Dave Williams and:

DECAPOLIS PUBLISHING